Discover Your Identity

Discover Your Identity

Real Stories from Real People to Inspire and Ignite Your Soul

Nothing of me is original. I am the combined effort of everyone I've ever known.

Chuck Palahniuk, *Invisible Monsters*

CONTENTS

Contents

INTRODUCTION

Today you are You,
That is truer than true.
There is no one alive
Who is Youer than You.

Dr. Seuss

**By Sue Brooke, founder and
co-creator of *Discover Your "I" Books***

Who are you? If your answer to that question involves anyone other than *you* (wife, mother, son, employee), then that is not *your* identity.

So what *is* your identity? Some say that it has something to do with your passion. So what does that mean?

Passion is the feeling you get when you're doing something that you absolutely love. It makes you smile. Your heart seems to race faster when you think about it. Your voice and eyes light up when you're talking about it, and when you're doing something you're passionate about, time doesn't seem to matter.

But what does that have to do with your identity? Everything! If you're living your passion, and doing what you love to do, then you've discovered who you really are!

We all struggle with our identity at one time or another. Oftentimes our identity changes as we go through the different "chapters" in our lives. Change is inevitable and just a part of our journey through our time on this earth.

As children, our identity is shaped largely on how, and with whom, we grow up: our environment, our family, and the events that surround our childhood. Those we spend the most time with as children are our first role models, and we tend to start our lives wanting to be just like them. As we grow and get older and our life experiences change, we learn more and more about ourselves. We discover what makes us smile, what we enjoy doing, and who we love to spend time with. We find the things we're good at, how our brains work, and the unique skills we have.

The people who touch our lives greatly shape our identity: our parents, siblings, family members, teachers, our relationships, friends, our children, the people we work with. Think back on your life and who may have influenced your identity at one time or another. How did this person affect who you are today?

As you read through the stories in this book, you will learn not only about each author's "story" on their road to discovering their identity as it is now, but hopefully they will inspire you to think about your own journey to *Discover Your Identity.*

With love,
Sue

By Susan Sheppard, founder and CEO of *Getting What You Want Publishing,* co-creator of *Discover Your "I" Books*

Would you consider that the identity of any one person changes from moment to moment? What is the source of our identity? Is it hereditary or environmental? These are all questions that have cluttered my brain since I was a child. I clearly remember, with fondness, a gathering in the living room of one of my grade school best friend's parents' home where we participated in an extensive debate about the determination of character being influenced more by heredity or environment. We never resolved the question, or determined a prevalent influence, but the conversation itself remained in the forefront of my memory until this day. So is character part of identity?

The study of human potential and self-improvement has been part of my life for almost forty years. I cannot say that there is any more clarity now than when I first entered the debate. There are things that have proven true to me, such as what you do is not who you are. Unfortunately, for many who accept that what they see is what is true, that is not always the case.

Many humans identify so strongly with their career and image that they are unable to separate their identity from their job. Your identity is self-created. It is a reflection of each person's values, beliefs, family, genetics, physical traits, environment, religious learnings, and personal experiences.

It is what allows a person to rise from the ghetto to positions of wealth and fame and power.

It is what allows tragedies caused by deviant leaders to occur.

It is an individual's identity that determines when they take a stand for something they believe in or when they cave to peer or power pressure in untenable situations.

Your identity is your heart and soul and the part of you that feels everything and the cumulative sensation of every moment of every single personal experience that you have ever lived.

We have gathered a series of stories depicting various incidents in a handful of real people's lives to hopefully touch a part of you that is buried deep inside of you, begging for attention in order for you to grow as a human being on your short visit to this earth. Some of our stories are lightweight, and others are profound and will rattle your core beliefs. I hope that one will touch you in a way that moves you.

Love,
Susan

ROCK STAR

Sue Brooke

Your time is limited, so don't waste it living someone else's life.

Steve Jobs

What did you want to be when you grew up? A fireman? A nurse? A superhero?

When I was a little girl, I wanted to be a rock star! But growing up in the middle of the cornfields of Nebraska, in a town like Mayberry, being a rock star or a movie star or just living in California was just not realistic. Those things just existed in the movies and on television. Back in those small towns, you're expected to go to college or take over the family business, which was usually a farm, get married and have kids, with a son to carry on the family name.

I don't remember my mother at all. She died from cancer on Christmas day when I was eight years old.

My sister was only five, so I immediately assumed the responsibility (identity) of being the oldest and having to cook, clean, and take care of myself and my sister.

We were raised by my father, a high school math teacher, who instilled in us the values and importance of education. We were taught to work hard and be responsible from a very young age. We showed horses, so doing chores at the crack of dawn, even in the dead of winter, and cleaning and taking care of the house and the animals was our "job."

My grandmother, though she and my grandfather lived in another town, became the female figure in my life and was the closest thing I had to a mother. She was a true entrepreneur, starting way back in the early 1900s. She and my grandfather had owned a popular steak house where everyone in the county came to eat, drink, and dance every weekend. My father and grandfather were both very kind and generous men, always there to help neighbors and friends. My grandmother was the foundation and strength that held the family together. I believe the combination of my giving father and the strength of my grandmother gave me the gift of becoming a strong, independent woman; they were the reason I became a teacher and an entrepreneur and eventually shaped what was to become my true identity.

From as early as I can remember, I wanted to be a teacher, just like my father. I loved going to his classroom after school, writing on the chalkboard and playing "school" with the neighbor kids on the weekends. I earned my teaching degree from the same college he graduated from with degrees in Elementary Education and Specific Learning Disabilities but did not begin my career as I had thought I would. I had a passion for dancing and, much to my father's chagrin, began teaching dance lessons for Fred Astaire Dance Studios.

I loved dancing, and being on stage kind of felt like being a rock star. I loved teaching dance and seeing how it made people feel physically, how it gave them confidence and made them smile. After learning how the business worked, I moved back to my college town, and at the age of twenty-four, I opened my first business, Ballroom Reflections Dance Studio.

Owning a business is also a little like being a rock star. You're in the public eye and people look up to you. It was the first time I truly felt what it was like to be "somebody," to be identified as a person of influence, and I must admit . . . it felt great!

Later, I sold my business, and against those small-town "odds," I got my first teaching job in . . . you guessed it . . . California! I didn't give up dancing, however, and began teaching line dancing at a local nightclub where I met the man who was to become my future husband. He was . . . you guessed it . . . a rock star! OK, so he wasn't exactly a rock star when I met him; he was in a band in Palm Springs, but he was very talented and had big dreams.

I quit my teaching job, moved closer to Los Angeles with him, and we began living our lives around the music business. I gave up my teaching career, and dancing, to focus on making his dreams of becoming a "real" rock star come true.

Artists and musicians are usually not what you might call "business people." They are creators, and most are happy just making music and performing, hence the stigma "starving artist"! My business sense came back quickly, and before long, he was becoming fairly well known in the "casual" music scene. While he wrote songs and performed at local venues, I spent my time learning how to get his songs onto CDs and how to market his music and build his fan base. I learned all about music copywriting and publishing, designed CD covers, developed his website, and found opportunities for him to perform, collaborate, produce, and record his own, as well as other people's, music.

Throughout our thirteen years together, it was a constant battle to convince him that he was "good enough," or handsome enough, or strong enough to "make it." I essentially became his psychologist, his best friend, his mother, and his wife—all morphed into one person. I'm not saying that's unusual in relationships, as I think that women tend to take on multiple roles for their husbands. The trick (as I eventually learned) is to not give up your identity in the process, which is precisely what I did.

Over those thirteen years, I was known as the "musician's wife." I spent every day trying to find ways to make *him* happy, make *him* successful . . . and make *his* dreams come true. Don't get me wrong . . . I loved my life and loved being a part of his career. I knew that I was an integral part of his success, and at the time, that was good enough for me.

My husband turned forty and, I guess you could say, went through that proverbial "midlife crisis." He chose to end our marriage after thirteen years, which left me devastated and distraught. I was bitter and sad and spent a lot of time trying to find ways to make him suffer the way I was suffering. One day, I was going through some old files and I found one of my journals. I had spent a lot of time alone while he was performing on the weekends, and I often spent those late nights writing while waiting up for him until the wee hours of the morning. There, in front of me, were the forgotten feelings that I had scribbled on those pages . . . I was lonely, I was sad . . . I had lost myself . . . I had lost my identity. I had lost *my* passion and forgotten *my* dreams. It was a subconscious choice at the time but a choice that consumed me . . . consumed my identity.

Shortly after the commencement of our divorce, I was hit by a truck . . . in more ways than one. A major car accident left me with a brain injury and multiple broken bones. I lay in that hospital bed believing that I had no friends—that all my friends had been his friends.

I had no identity of my own because I had been known for thirteen years as "the musician's wife." My dreams had left along with him, and I felt lost and alone.

Then it happened . . . I opened my eyes in that hospital room and before me was a room full of people—people who were there because they cared about *me*. They were there because I meant something to them. The feeling was overwhelming, and it was that very moment that changed my life forever.

During my year of recovery, my broken jaw was wired shut, I walked with a cane to my daily physical therapy, and I was going through a difficult divorce. Suddenly my bank account was depleted, and I was financially devastated at age forty-four. I had a big decision to make: I could just give up or make the choice to be the rock star I always wanted to be.

Fast forward to today . . . I have built a successful business all by myself. I found a passion for inspiring people through writing and speaking, and my dreams of inspiring people and encouraging them to see their life challenges as amazing opportunities has come true. Everything that I had experienced turned out to be the *best* thing that could have ever happened!

Whatever happened to my "rock star" ex-husband? Well, he appeared ten years later after he divorced my ex-friend whom he had left me for. We had long conversations about the years we spent together and the events surrounding the demise of our marriage. He said the words I longed to hear, which made everything fall perfectly into place. He said, "It was because of *you* that I've had the successes that I have. It was because of *you* that I am who I am today. I made a big mistake and I'm sorry."

No, I did not go back to him. We parted ways and I truly hope the best for him. I was finally graced with the gift of appreciation and respect. Few people are fortunate enough to have that kind of closure, so for that, I am eternally grateful.

I know now that I should have never given up my dreams of becoming a rock star, but everything happened exactly as it was supposed to, at exactly the right time. I may not be wearing spandex and dancing and singing on stage with a band, but I can still be a different kind of rock star: inspiring others to become anything they want to be, to never lose their identity, and to never give up on their dreams, no matter how crazy they may seem!

About the Author

Sue Brooke is the founder and creator of the Discover Your "I" book series, a small-business owner, speaker, educator, author, coach, and idea innovator! After surviving a car accident and finding herself with a depleted bank account at the age of forty-four, Sue describes "being hit by a truck" as the moment that changed her life forever. She reclaimed her identity after giving it up to manage her former husband's music career and built a successful business all on her own. Sue is a passionate advocate for anyone who may have lost their identity, or given up on their dreams, to empower and inspire them to live their passion and never give up on their dreams, no matter how crazy they may seem!

Visit her online at http://www.SueBrooke.com and http://www.DiscoverYourI.com.

TO BE OR NOT TO BE ME

Susan Sheppard

A girl should be two things:
who and what she wants.

Coco Chanel, *The Gospel According to Coco Chanel:*
Life Lessons from the World's Most Elegant Woman

It was 1959, and at that moment, I wanted to be a boy with all my heart!

Let me give a little history.

1943, November 5, at 5:03 p.m., I was born to Elmer and Lorraine Spychala.

In 1945, my sister Judy arrived, then

1948, my brother Jim came,

1950, my sister Janet made her entrance,

1955, my brother Michael was next, and finally

1957, along came my brother Tom.

My dad was an electrician. My mother was a stay-at-home mom. Every time another child arrived, I watched my dad do something amazing to take care of our family. He was a very beautiful and talented man. I wanted to be like him and take on challenges when they appeared.

When Jim came, my dad built an addition on the house.

About the time Janet arrived, I remember sitting in the basement watching my dad as he soldered all the little tiny wires and put in the television tubes to build our first television while he attended electronics school. I was blissfully unaware that there was a gender difference when it came to taking on challenges.

In 1955 after Mike joined us, Dad took a year off from work to build a five-bedroom house for our growing family. He did the carpentry, plumbing, and electrical work himself, only hiring contractors for expertise. This was so impressive to me. It just reinforced my desire to create value in the world.

In 1957, we moved into that amazing brick house in Grayslake that my dad had actually built, and I started high school.

I was an honor student, but intentionally I did my best to not be at the top of the class, because I didn't want to be a nerd. I wasn't a cheerleader or the most popular; nor was I a jock or one of the girls who hung out with the Fonzie types in leather jackets.

I was friendly with everyone and somewhat invisible. I didn't really know what I was going to do with my life other than not live in a small town. Obviously I was destined to do something, since I was pressured by my parents and teachers to get good grades and take college prep courses.

I really liked to take things apart and figure out how they worked, so in my junior year, I decided to take a class in mechanical drawing. To my surprise, I was told girls were not allowed to take mechanical drawing. This was my first rude awakening to the inequities between the sexes. The school board, composed entirely of men, vetoed my petition for the class and recommended home economics.

I didn't understand why "because I was a girl" I couldn't take a class in something that interested me. I thought this was a free country.

Oblivious as to what was yet to be revealed, I argued that I wanted to become a mechanical engineer. My dad laughed and dismissed my idea as an excuse to hang out with boys.

I was really struggling with the ambivalent messages that were bombarding me. Be smart, but you are a girl, so you can't do what you want. Study hard so you can get married and have babies and not go to college.

Who am I and what am I supposed to do?

When I asked my parents to complete the financials in a college application, their response was my biggest shock. There are three boys and three girls in this family. In our opinion, you girls do not need a higher education, since you will have a husband to support you. This offended me in my soul! I couldn't imagine the idea of not being able to have the career that I wanted or to be able to take care of myself.

I was horrified! What was different? Because I was female, I couldn't have a career?

They explained that college was never in the plan for the girls. The insurance policy in my name, worth $2,000 at maturity, was to pay for a wedding.

The boys need careers because they will have families to support, so their insurance policies would mature to $20,000 for their educations.

This is that moment in 1959 where I wanted to be a boy more than anything else I could imagine.

Girls were not as valuable as boys! That determined my dilemma. How could I go to college on $2,000? As sure as hell, I wasn't getting married instead of going to college!

After much crying and begging, my dad finally consented that an acceptable avenue for his daughter was to be a teacher or a nurse. I researched all the possibilities.

I didn't want to be a teacher, so I started to explore nursing. It wasn't appealing to me, except for the science classes, and I would get to meet a lot of people. If I went to a three-year school to become a registered nurse that was affiliated with a university, I could get college credit for all the science courses. Evanston Hospital affiliated with Northwestern University, and it looked like just one more year and I could have a degree in biology or psychology. The total cost for the three-year, year-round program, including room and board, was $2,000.

I was sure this was the answer. My GPA got me entrance to Northwestern, but here was the bad news: I really hated nursing school.

The science classes were good, but the nursing classes were horrible. I didn't like being subservient, having to stand up when doctors walked in the room, following orders, changing beds, and giving people bed baths.

There was no choice; I had to stick it out. So I did, graduating by the skin of my teeth.

I was in trouble most of the time I was in nursing school, not for bad grades, but I was a bit of a rebel. I had a very difficult time being in an all-female school that felt like a convent. The NU girls were wearing mini-skirts, and we wore starched pinafore uniforms with hems measured 12" from the ground that looked like nun's habits.

The director and I rarely saw eye to eye on anything. So until the day of graduation my senior year, I wasn't sure I was even going to graduate.

Finally, in 1964, I became a registered nurse. I wanted to continue to go to school, but there was no more money. If I got a job as a nurse, I could continue my education and pay for it myself. Then no one could tell me what I could or couldn't do.

Only thirty-five college credits were transferable from Northwestern University, because none of those nursing classes counted for college credit, so it was three more years of expensive college to graduate.

A hospital job was obvious. I enjoyed the patients and learning about their medical problems and saving lives. I made a list of all the things I really wouldn't tolerate in a job. Bed baths, passing hundreds of medications to patients that I didn't know, and charting people's bowel movements and sleep habits were on the list.

The solution was two places—the operating room and the emergency room.

In the operating room, the patients are unconscious, it's claustrophobic, breathing fresh air would be rare, and it's freezing cold.

In the emergency room, unpredictability, chaos, and interaction with people from the outside world were the norm. Also, there was autonomy because the emergency-room nurses evaluated the patient's first and directed the patient flow. Then I remembered, as a student in the emergency room, my picture appeared on the front page of the *Chicago Sun-Times* with a Brink's guard who was shot during a robbery in the hospital.

Was fame a possibility? Obviously, emergency was my choice. The challenge was inspiring.

It became my goal to be one of the best ER nurses that I could possibly be, to develop my intuition, to be in touch with the patients, to learn the latest treatments and technology, and to be respected by my peers and by the doctors. This truly was a step in the direction I had not expected to go.

It was the development of my identity as a woman of power, who happened to be a nurse.

I spent forty years saving lives, stamping out disease, preventing pain and suffering, and contributing to the communities that we served. In addition to learning crisis intervention and how to be a really great manager of a team, I found myself to be an influential woman who made a difference.

In 2014, I celebrated my fifty-year career as a registered nurse in many hospitals, in many capacities, doing what I love best: making a difference for spiritual beings having a human experience on this earth.

As an ER/ICU administrator, I learned to expect more from my employees than they thought they could produce, and they often achieved goals that were beyond their own expectations.

Ironically, my twenty-three-year marriage to a wonderful man who was a Vietnam vet suffering from PTSD ended in divorce. Those years, as well as another twenty-plus years as a single mom, required my financial support for our family, which would not have been possible without my RN and my later BS degree in business that I paid for myself.

I have moved on. Now I help people with wounded hearts to heal and find love. It's just another way to complement my own identity, which is to make a difference in the world as a healer and an influencer.

About the Author

Susan Sheppard is the founder of Getting What You Want, Inc., a life and relationship coaching organization created to teach sacred intimacy in all personal relationships. She is the author of the books *How to Get What You Want from Your Man Anytime* and *Dating after 40: No More Excuses* and *Romance Re-Entry for Those Out of Practice.*

Susan's forty years as a registered nurse in emergency services has honed her crisis-intervention skills as a coach, author, and speaker whose mission is to replace fear with love by her courageous conversations, inspired writing, and honesty. She is on a mission to get people loved the way they want to be loved. She has a track record of helping people meet their perfect partner and find true intimacy, love, and commitment.

She has been a partner or founder of nine different businesses in many different industries and is truly a renaissance woman.

You can visit Susan at http://www.GettingWhatYouWant.com.

MAMA'S GIRL

Karen Strauss

It is easier to live through someone else than to complete yourself. The freedom to lead and plan your own life is frightening if you have never faced it before. It is frightening when a woman finally realizes that there is no answer to the question "who am I" except the voice inside herself.

Betty Friedan

"Karen, come here!" My mother's angry voice beckoned me to the living room once again. This time, she was prepared with a stack of photographs from magazines and newspapers of fat and obese women. She says, "You see this?! This is you in ten pounds."

This was just another tactic, in a series of tactics, to tell me how overweight and unattractive I was. She would cajole, bully, and put me on every diet known to mankind in those days—not to mention drag me to Queens every so often to have my naturally curly hair

17

straightened. And when I was seventeen, she convinced me I needed a nose job.

Oddly enough, I was actually pretty popular in high school—had lots of friends, was president of the Drama Club, and enjoyed an active social life. I was in honors classes all through high school and, by all accounts, seemed like a confident, well-adjusted young woman. Perhaps I was a little too vocal for my teachers and high school principal—but nothing out of the ordinary or too extreme.

My self-esteem, however, was permanently bruised, and I was convinced I would never be able to have a normal relationship with a man, as I was too fat and unlovable.

I had a "boyfriend" in high school . . . I snuck out of the house to drive the car to Brooklyn, which was a big deal coming from Long Island. My mother, of course, did not like him, which made me like him even more. In looking back, however, he never "tried" anything with me, and he was four years older than me. My feeling now is that he was probably gay.

My mother's voice continued to be in my head for many years. It affected every relationship I ever had with men when I was in my twenties. The choices I made were horrible: these were not good men. I just chose men who were like my mother . . . verbally abusive. It was what I was used to and familiar with. I didn't even recognize a pattern.

My mother died when I was thirty. She was only fifty-nine when she was diagnosed with a brain tumor . . . a grade-four glioblastoma. She was one year younger than I am now.

This was a major turning point in my life. I went through a year of complete turmoil and confusion, grieving for a woman I didn't get along with and grieving for a relationship that would now never happen. I went through a serious depression and sought psychological help, as I did not know what was happening to me. Ironically, I wound up losing thirty pounds and became the "hot babe." This new body shape and growing popularity really took me out of my comfort zone. It confused me even more. I had no mentors, no mother figure, my father was too far gone in his grief to focus on his children, and my women friends were in party mode.

The only place I was confident and comfortable was at work. I could be myself—smart, articulate, and creative—without having to physically impress someone. No one was judging me on my looks when I presented ideas at work, especially when I started my own company at age thirty-five.

Eventually I went through intense therapy, took anti-depressants, and started dating men who were like my father. They were introspective, kind, and supportive, but unbeknownst to me then, passive-aggressive. One man wooed me relentlessly. He was consistent in his calling, asking me out, treating me like a lady, and constantly complimenting me. He even told me I had "breasts for the world"!

But after dating awhile, he was uninterested in taking it to the next level. Instead of talking to me about it, he just became "unavailable," stopped calling so much, and broke promises. In the end, he forced me to break up with him. That's what passive-aggressive people do. They don't confront you, but instead by their inaction, they make you so mad that you are forced to take action and be the bad guy.

I was now left in a state of confusion, anxiety, and depression. I blamed this all on the fact that I was too fat and unlovable. Of course, this was all in my head, but it was very real to me.

The final blow for me was when I met the man who I was sure would be my future husband. I never felt so loved, so safe, so taken care of as when I was with Bob. He embraced my physicality and made me feel like the most beautiful woman in the world. We talked of marriage as soon as he was divorced. Yes, he was separated from his wife when I met him. They had two daughters in high school and had been married more than twenty years. What a fool I was to believe him. In the end, his wife and daughters pleaded with him to come back, and being the passive-aggressive man he was, that's what he did. He didn't have the courtesy to tell me until after he moved back in with his family.

Again, it must have been my fault. I was unlovable . . . why else would he pick a woman he was unhappy with and choose an unfulfilling marriage over the woman he supposedly loved best in the world—me? But it was not meant to be, and once again, I was alone with my unproductive and negative thoughts.

So what changed? How did I shake my unshakable belief that I was too fat to be loved and unlovable in every way?

I did it with help from my therapists in understanding that the dynamic between my mother and my father, the idea of emotional abandonment, and a failure of my mother and me to bond properly all brought on these beliefs of inadequacy. My therapists helped me understand what happened to me and helped me understand that this was not my fault. They also helped me see that my choices in men were only fostering my negative beliefs about myself.

I am still a work in progress. For many years, I preferred to be alone. I always had great friends, great work, and a job in which I travelled a lot and met many interesting people, so I wasn't lonely. It is recently that I am now in a place where I understand, intellectually, and now even emotionally, that I am a woman of value. I have a lot to give to a potential partner, and most of all, I am ready to receive. I have surrounded myself with positive and supportive people. I have managed to get rid of most of the toxic people in my life, and that has made a huge difference.

I wake up feeling good about myself, my life, and my prospects for the future. I feel I have finally gotten to the core of my identity . . . of who I really am!

About the Author

Karen Strauss is a publishing veteran with broad experience in all aspects of sales, marketing, strategic planning, and distribution.

Strauss is publisher of RockStar Publishing House. Designed to publish books from entrepreneurs and self-publishing authors, RockStar is a one-stop-shop publisher who will edit, design, distribute, and help market your book.

Strauss Consultants works with small- and medium-size publishers to maximize sales to the largest retailers and wholesalers in the country. For further information, go to http://www.rockstar publishinghouse.com or http://www.straussconsultants.com.

MY TRUE IDENTITY

Joe DiChiara

*To be yourself in a world that
is constantly trying to make
you something else is the
greatest accomplishment.*

Ralph Waldo Emerson

When I was presented with the opportunity to write
a chapter for this book, I thought that I would simply
write about who I am and how I got here. Pretty simple, right? Wrong! As I sat down to start typing, I realized that it may be a good idea to look up the definition
of the word instead of assuming that I knew what it
meant. This is significant and a very good example of
what my identity is today. I will explain what I mean by
this at the end of the chapter.

This is from Dictionary.com:

IDENTITY—

1: the state or fact of remaining the same one or ones, as under varying aspects or conditions:

The identity of the fingerprints on the gun with those on file provided evidence that he was the killer.

2: the condition of being oneself or itself, and not another.

He doubted his own identity.

I believe, like everyone else in the world, my identity is evolving. The identity I own today probably won't be the same identity next year, simply because I choose to keep learning and progressing. Hopefully my future self will be a little kinder and gentler; I will be more patient and more understanding. Who I am today is not who I was three, five, or ten years ago. There are many people that are very, very grateful for that.

I believe that, like most people, my identity began taking shape the moment I was born and was greatly influenced by my family. We don't get to choose who our family is; that decision was made by a higher authority. Their perceptions, misperceptions, beliefs, routines, habits, talents, and so on, are all handed down, both intentionally and unintentionally. Unfortunately, right or wrong, those early lessons are ingrained so deeply into our core that we are driven by them without even realizing it.

Why does laziness and inactivity gnaw at me to a point of working myself to exhaustion? Did it have anything to do with seeing my dad spend years lying on the couch watching television and smoking four packs of Marlboros a day instead of getting a job and supporting us? Why was it so important for me to try to be an early riser when my body chemistry could never adapt and then feeling like a failure and beating myself up over it? Did my grandfather's habits have any effect on my perception of what hard work was? Gramps would get to bed early, wake up early, and never missed a day of work in his life. The answer I found out was . . . Absolutely! All of this affected my thinking and my perception of how the world worked.

The truth is that it's OK to lie on the couch and watch television once in a while. That doesn't make you lazy. The truth is that I'm most productive at night, and getting up at the crack of dawn was counterproductive to actually running my business. These awakenings are what my coach, Maryann Ehmann, calls "false beliefs." My life, my perceptions of the world, my identity were being affected by perceived truths that nobody knowingly taught me. It was what I saw as a child, and it was ingrained into my subconscious so deeply that undoing those false beliefs took years. They aren't lies. Getting up early was what worked for Gramps. My father wasn't lazy, or maybe he was, I don't know. I do know that he suffered from an untreated gambling addiction, depression, and a four-pack-a-day smoking habit. Learning these facts has helped me understand my gene pool and, more important, that I don't have to take on those self-destructive habits my dad suffered from or even follow my grandfather's routines. I can be my own true self: the person I was meant to be.

The Truth

I was blessed with a very loving, close family. My parent's first child and my grandparent's first grandchild . . . I was special. At least in their eyes I was, and they definitely made me feel that way. I was "The Little Man," and they touted me (at least I believed they did) to my large extended family as "the one that's going to make it big." If my family believed that, or not, wasn't the issue. I believed it. And most of my life, I carried the self-imposed burden of being "the one" that was going to lift up my entire clan and bring them to the Promised Land. I was the first to realize "the American Dream." I was told at an early age that "you can do anything you set your mind to." I could be the president of the United States if I wanted to be! I decided I was going to be 6'2" and play centerfield for the New York Yankees. I still have not given up on that dream, and I don't know how, but it's going to happen . . . maybe just not the way I thought it would. I'll keep you posted on that.

Born in 1960, I was too young to be drafted and serve in Vietnam but not too young to see the carnage on television every night and not too young to overhear my parents talking about bringing me to Canada if this went on much longer. I was too young to experience things like Woodstock but not too young to hear about heroin addicts hanging out in our building. These were all images and tidbits that molded my identity and contributed to those false beliefs.

Between the ages of seven and ten, we lived on Madison Street in New York City. A three-room (not bedrooms) apartment with one bedroom, a kitchen where the bathtub was located (no shower), and a living room where the bathroom was. This was one of the better apartments, because all the other ones had bathrooms out in the hallway. There were six of us when we moved out in 1970 . . . two adults and four children in a three-room apartment, and it was one of the happiest times in my life. It was normal to me, and it was normal to my dad because he grew up in the building.

We lived blocks away from "Little Italy," and my dad's heroes growing up were all the mob guys from the neighborhood. His goal in life, when he was young, was to be a like them. To be a "made man" was an honor. I think that changed when he met my mom, but he always idolized them. The truth was that those guys all live miserable lives, filled with tragedy after tragedy. Most of them are broke, living day to day, and neglecting their families. They are hypocrites that go to church in the morning and murder at night. My dad didn't see it that way. He was taught that they were important people and were well respected.

That shaped his identity and helped shaped mine. I grew up detesting those people, because I thought they were a negative influence on my dad. I made it a point to be honest and faithful. It made me try, as best as I could, to be true to my word and build a lasting, positive legacy for my family. It made me want to be a real, positive example, at home and at work—to be transparent, no matter where I was. So the first fifty years of my life were shaped by the obvious influences, both good and bad . . . family, friends, clients, mentors, coaches. All contributed to what I now call my false identity. It was false because some of it was based on a lot of false beliefs. For instance, when I was seventeen and my grandmother said, "I don't like the guys you're hanging around with." Now I understand that what she meant was to find better people to associate with, and they will help you be better. Grandma was right, because most of my immediate crowd in high school went to prison. Today, I gravitate toward people like you that read books like this.

In the first paragraph, I mentioned the fact that looking up the definition of "identity" was significant— the reason being that I understand today that I don't know everything, so I don't assume anything, and I am very comfortable with that. Not "knowing" was a sign of weakness, and today, asking, for me, is a sign of strength. Maybe ten years ago, I would have looked up the definition but never told anyone about it. Today I've shared it on the chance that it could make a small difference in your life. It's my way of teaching what was taught to me . . . Pay it forward. This is how I am coming to know and understand who I really am and what my true identity is. I used to think I was a father, a CPA, a business owner . . . I know today, my true role is to be a teacher and a student enrolled in the Universal University with God as the principal. When I pursue my God-given talents and interest, I am getting closer to my true identity.

This part of the definition resonates with me:

2: The condition of being oneself or itself, and not another.

I believe that my true identity is revealed when I am doing something where time stands still. I call it being in "The Zone"—a time when nothing matters except what I am doing right in this instant. It's very easy to identify those times. Time stands still for me when I am teaching, learning and evolving, and sharing my God-given talents and experience with others. Those are the times I feel that I am one with God and when I am closest to my true self.

About the Author

Born to be an entrepreneur, Mr. **Joe DiChiara** opened his first CPA office in 1994 and has worked with thousands of small-business owners over the past thirty-plus years. He enjoys sharing his unique experience and knowledge with entrepreneurs that desire business and financial success.

A proud father of three adult children, he loves teaching, learning, traveling, and experiencing life. His favorite jobs are cleaning his room and walking his dog, Winston, when he is home.

To learn more about Mr. DiChiara, visit http://www.joedichiara.biz and http://www.bedrockbookkeepersonlineacademy.com.

LITTLE GIRL LOST AND FOUND

Bonnie Romero

The thing women have yet to learn is nobody gives you power. You just take it.

Roseanne Barr

I woke up one morning in the middle of the summer of 1982 and heard my mother crying like I had never heard her cry before. This was a sound like someone had died. This was a pain that I never wanted to feel. She was leaning over the kitchen sink and sobbing. I asked her, "Are you hurt?" She told me, "The pain I feel, you cannot take away."

My dad said, with his deep voice, "Bonnie, come here, I need to speak to you."

I walked over to my dad as he popped the door open from the bathroom with his large, brown cowboy boot. That image is so intense in my mind to this day as if it were yesterday. I knew there was something very bad about to happen in my life when he looked down at me and said, "I will always love you, and if you want to stay here with me, you can, for as long as you want."

My dad had never told me he loved me before that day. My mother screamed, from the top of her lungs, that I was not his daughter, and this would be the last time he would ever see me.

I was twelve years old, and for a minute, it seemed like my life had ended. In actuality, my life had ended as I knew it. I found out that my biological father was really a homeless alcoholic. I always wondered about him after that and what he looked like. Did he love me? Why didn't he want me? I never felt a real, true love from my mom that little girls should feel. My mom suffered from depression. I was an only child and entertained myself with my dog, Clyde, most of the time, climbing trees and playing with the boys.

There was a little boy next door named Jamie. I always had a secret crush on him. He is the one who broke the news to me that he saw my stepdad with another woman.

It is such a cliché that the woman my stepdad had an affair with, and left my mom for, was his secretary. My stepdad ended up marrying her, and they are still married today.

My mom and I moved to Huntington Park, California, east of Los Angeles, that summer, from the little town of Kingman, Arizona. I had to leave my best friends, Gina and Dawna, which was tragic for me.

Moving to a big city was exciting, as I had always visited my Aunt Diane, who lived in California, and we would go to fun places. We moved in with my aunt and her girlfriend. I thought of California as my front yard being the beach and movie stars and Disneyland being in my backyard.

I started school at Huntington Park Gage Junior High, and it was a full Hispanic community. There were a total of four white students, including myself. The kids would pick on me and take my lunch. I would cry every day. Soon I befriended gang members that took me under their wings. They taught me to fight and would protect me from other students who would pick on me.

In December 1984, we had my Christmas dance at school. A boy named Albert asked me to dance to a song called "Careless Whisper" by Wham!. I danced with him because all the girls liked him, and he wanted me. This was going to be payback to all the hater-girls who were mean to me. I was the lucky one, or so I thought. There was something about him . . . he made me laugh and kissed really well. He made me feel like I was the prettiest girl in the world. He was always a charmer, and he could tell you anything you wanted to hear.

After one week's time, I walked home from school with him, to his house, where we started making out in the backseat of his sister's car in the driveway.

I was afraid that he would leave me if I didn't go further with him, and I didn't want him to leave me—like my stepdad left my mother. We had sex that night in his room, and I remember thinking in my mind . . . I will be with him forever now. This is what you do, right? You stay with the person you love. You marry them and live happily ever after.

Shortly thereafter, things started to change. He wanted me to go home straight from school, and I could no longer have friends because they didn't like him. He thought they put bad thoughts in my head about him.

I had to answer the phone when he would call me. I was no longer allowed to do anything unless it was with him.

The physical abuse started about a year after we were together. I was talking to a boy in my class about an assignment, and Albert saw me. It was an innocent conversation, but he wasn't having that. When class was over, Albert slapped me across the face.

Somehow or another, he twisted it around, and the next thing I knew I was apologizing and saying I wouldn't do it again.

I should have turned around and ran the other way then, but I didn't. I loved him. I thought it was only one time . . . that would never happen again. He only slapped me because he was jealous and loved me, right?

My mom and aunt hated Albert. In 1986, we moved to Culver City, California. My mom thought this would get me away from him and also the gangs.

I would ditch school to be with him, eventually running away with him, becoming pregnant with my son, and marrying this man. I knew I had turned into an abused woman at this point, totally under his control.

Around 1990, Albert started doing a drug called speed, better known today as methamphetamine. Once he started taking this drug, he never stopped and eventually had to steal to provide for this habit. It started in a pill form, and then he would snort it, eventually turning to smoking it to satisfy the addiction that his body craved. I couldn't help him with this addiction, as I had never actually taken drugs myself, and I certainly couldn't give him the high that this drug did. Our entire life was brought down because of it.

I just wanted a normal life and thought of Nicole Brown Simpson and how O. J. killed her after she finally left him. I endured many beatings, but one night I said, "I am done."

I couldn't deal with Albert's paranoia, mood swings, and lack of money. I suffered beatings every time I would question him about where he was or the girls he was cheating on me with.

Soon I was pregnant with my daughter and didn't want to bring another child into my dark, depressing life. I was so ashamed of what I had allowed my life to become . . . nothing.

One day Albert saw I was leaving him. He backhanded me so hard in my right ear that I flew across the room. My ear was pulsing and hot and making a ringing noise. Albert then started banging my head into the ground saying, "Why did you do this to me? Why do you make me so angry that I have to hurt you?"

He coldly told me that I was not going anywhere, that he would kill me first. I begged him to stop.

Finally, after he was out of breath and had no more strength, he stopped. When he left in the car, I told myself I would win if I killed myself before he had the pleasure and chance of doing it himself.

I started slicing my wrists, but they burned, and it hurt so bad that I was tired of hurting. I considered driving off the freeway overpass that night, but thank goodness Albert never brought my car back that night.

That same night, I had prayed, and also yelled at God, and by the morning, peace had entered my heart because I heard God answer me. God told me to leave my situation and not look back. God also told me to tell my mother and aunt everything.

I left Albert, and I never looked back. I returned to school and even graduated from the police academy; I also obtained a BA in Criminology. I took the control back in my life and am happily married and have a full-time career. I also enjoy being a stand-up comedian on the side, as it is healing. I am currently working on a book about my life story, as there is so much more to be told. I now speak to women in abuse shelters, sharing hope.

My identity? I was a little girl lost, but now I'm found.

About the Author

Bonnie Romero is a mother, wife, grandma, and a survivor of domestic abuse.

She is a stand-up comedian, sales rep, author, and a public speaker in regard to going from desperation to inspiration.

Bonnie loves people and her job and works in sales for a huge commercial trucking dealership and has been with her company for eighteen years.

Bonnie is currently working on an autobiography that will be out by next year that you will not want to miss out on. It will talk about being an only child, growing up in small town, and moving to huge city where she learned to be tough only to become a battered lonely wife after marrying her ex-husband, who was physically abusive and a drug addict. You will see the pain she went through and how she overcame suicidal thoughts and ultimately survived and found herself. Bonnie learned how to laugh and love again and become successful in her career. She will show you how she went from codependent to independent.

Her hobbies are dancing, singing karaoke, and traveling.

A CHANGE OF TUNE

Melody Breyer-Grell

Be yourself; everyone else is already taken.

Oscar Wilde

When I was a young girl, between seven and ten, I had a routine. After school, I would retrieve ten pennies from my coat pocket. Then they would be inserted into the slot of a round, glass gum machine. I would arrive home to my family's large, airy apartment. (We lived in a brand new working-class housing development in Queens.) Once in my room, the door closed, I would read until dinner—mostly children's fiction. And chew gum . . . Bliss!

A couple of times a year, we would get an application from Scholastic Publications to buy these books. I was always pleasantly surprised when my mother permitted me to get the amount I requested . . . considerably more than my other schoolmates. Although she claimed that we were poor, it did not hinder my acquisition of a large personal library. And, of course, there was the public library. I spent much time alone in my room, reading, but all my desires were met.

Only when we moved to Long Island (my parents having chosen a house bordering a rich neighborhood) did I began to feel lonely.

My situation had changed drastically. Though I was eager to start school, I was shut out, as the other girls, mostly well dressed and comfortable with each other, chose to leave me out of their activities. But I did have something most of them did not . . . an outstanding soprano voice.

Not that it made my life any easier, for my mother decided it was time for me to make my "debut." Every time she would have friends over, she would have (make) me sing for them. I squirmed as I warbled "The Sound of Music" for the zillionth time. And when she sent a note to my homeroom teacher, suggesting that I get up and sing for the class, I was mortified, humiliated, and ultimately bullied into performing. I had to forgive her because she did not understand the effects of such pushing. Not being musical herself, she thought any talent was "magic."

Although I was initially resistant to singing, I did succumb to the beauty of Rodgers and Hammerstein and the operas of Puccini, Verdi, and Mozart. I was always testing my range and power, to see what I could do, fearlessly, for I did not believe I would be a professional singer. I thought it was a whim; I was too reckless for the voice to last.

I also needed to be the "best." With no care of forming healthy relationships with people in school, I was the diva. To sing louder, higher, and more beautifully than anyone else—that was all that mattered. I did have a couple of friends, other singers, and of course, my coterie of gay buddies. I did not realize why those boys did not like me the way I wanted to be liked. Such a cliché for a girl in the arts!

I sang my way into a full music scholarship, leaving home to attend the Curtis Institute of Music. While setting up my apartment with my ever-helpful mother, I felt dissociated.

"Why am I here?" I asked her. "What do I expect to get?" Surprisingly and uncharacteristically, my mother agreed with me and understood my doubts.

My feelings were well founded. For according to some instructors, I was not a musician at all, just a person with a voice, some stage presence, and confidence. You might think that was enough, but for Curtis it was not, due to the heavy course load. There was also much political dissension to contend with, as my teacher, new that year, was roundly hated (for good reason) by the others. Bad karma abounded, so I just went to scores of parties and accelerated my demise.

By the end of my first year at Curtis, I was put on probation. I decided not to return. I knew that I was not meant to be a theoretician, play an instrument, or take two-part dictation, as was part of the program. My surviving Curtis was not in the cards. That is one thing that I am sure of until this day. There was another plan for me. And it was a long time in coming.

While floundering around in New York City, I got married to solve all my problems. It was not a random choice, and we are married still. Of course, matrimony itself did not bring me peace, so I acted a bit, but my fluctuating weight limited my repertoire.

It was a clear spring day (one of those rare times between chill and heat), and I was bopping down West End Avenue. My sister had lent me her CD of Ella Fitzgerald singing Duke Ellington. I formed a manic desire to sing this music, even though I had zero background in jazz.

Against the advice of teachers and coaches, I plunged into this new world, determined to make a life singing jazz. I practiced every day, and I even cranked out a well-reviewed CD. But my efforts were tremendously draining emotionally and financially, as I had to pay the band. My job now (that I could sing the music) was to secure gigs in cabaret and jazz clubs. Sure, it was nice if one was "good" in those rarefied circles, but there was a lot more to it. One needed to fill seats and be able to finesse contacts with a disciplined manner. Like a broken thermostat, I tried too hard or slacked off. I was not in it for the long haul.

But before I hung up my microphone, I had something to say. My frustration with the music business led me to pick up my pencil and create a parody show—*What's So Funny About Jazz?* The lyrics lampoon the often humorless treatment of an originally loose art form. The writing of those lyrics came naturally to me; I was fearless and funny. Then I hung it all up and got myself a dog.

To be a successful singer, a performer, to "make it," requires certain prerequisites that I never had . . . a focus, an identity, a cohesive, singular vision of what was up for sale. An opera singer or a jazz singer needs to be able to work in a group with musicians and musical directors. I was not that person, voice or not. For me, singing was a compulsion, not a vocation. After a burnout, I finally could see that I was an introvert and bookworm who merely needed some alone time.

Just a few weeks into the process of training my dog, Nora, I received a call from a former producer, a colleague of mine, asking me to review some singers' CDs for his website.

"Why would I do that?"

"Because," he said, "you are a writer." He had heard my parodies.

After I had agreed, he played hard to get. When he did not send me the CDs needed to make good on his offer, I snuck into his office, nabbed a disk, and sent him a review. He put it up. Because I was no longer singing, editors and publishers believed I was conversant enough in music to write about it. I wrote . . . not only about music but about whatever caught my interest. My reviews and interviews were published in *Cabaret Scenes* magazine and the *Huffington Post* blog. I have placed stories in several anthologies: fiction, memoir, and romance.

It was not long before I became immersed in the craft of writing. My earlier voracious reading had propped me up and wired my brain for it. I set out to master the technical aspects of correct grammar (I am still working on it) because, for the first time, I enjoyed the theoretical aspects of an art form.

I love the writing life. It is a rich, yet solitary, existence . . . the one that I was born to do. I am thrilled if I get published but understand when I don't. (Well, sort of!)

My voice had found itself, at last, in a profession I could approach concurrently with enthusiasm and humility. It does not matter if I am having a bad hair day or what I am wearing, and I don't have to leave my house to do it.

We don't write with the clear intention of making money. If you want money, become an IT guy or gal. But if you are a writer, gold can be mined, even with a half-hour break from "real" life.

About the Author

Melody Breyer Grell, originally a singer, made her professional writing debut with lyrics to her satirical *What's So Funny About Jazz?* She was soon on board with *Cabaret Scenes* magazine, writing reviews, interviews, and features.

Melody's fiction, essays, and memoirs have been published in various anthologies and journals. They include *The Fairhaven Literary Review*, *The Cat's Meow*, and short "romance" stories featured in *Counting Down the Seconds* and *SunKissed* (both published in the United Kingdom by Freya Publications). Breyer-Grell is a frequent contributor to *The Huffington Post*—opining on a broad range of subjects—from peace in the Middle East to *American Idol*.

Melody's essay "Just Say No" appears in the 2015 release of the anthology *Dumped: Women Defriending Women*, edited by Nina Gaby.

CAN A PLASTIC BOWL CHANGE YOUR LIFE?

Nicole Rhoades

Never forget what you are, for surely the world will not. Make it your strength. Then it can never be your weakness. Armour yourself in it, and it will never be used to hurt you.

George R. R. Martin, *A Game of Thrones*

Have you ever thought, "You *are* what you do?"

I was an activity director for a very large community in Las Vegas, Nevada, for many years. It was "who" I was. It was "what" I did. I was proud that I was able to work my schedule around my three children, two stepkids, and my husband. When I was at work, I could bring my kids to activities so they were not home alone, I was able to bring my new puppy to work and trained her there, and to top it off, I made a very substantial income doing what I loved. This was the ideal job for me, and I loved what I did. Why would I want to do anything else?

47

Suddenly, without any warning, the rug was pulled out from under me. I got a call from the corporate office telling me they were closing my activity center that very same day. Frantically, I thought, "What am I going to do? Who is going to hire me? How do I find a job that I can work around my kids' schedules and make the amount of money I make?"

I was shocked and saddened as I cleaned out my office and locked the doors to my center for the very last time. I knew unemployment benefits wouldn't suffice, with five kids at home and bills to pay. Mostly, I was sad that all the people at the community center wouldn't have a community center any longer; I would no longer be a part of their families as I had been for years, and that broke my heart.

My family was sympathetic, of course, when they heard the news. After all, it was their community center as well, and of course, my husband's thoughts went directly to money. How can we pay our bills without my income? He quickly reminded me that the lease on my minivan was coming due shortly, and I had to have a job with the same kind of income in just a few short months.

I called my good friend Jane, looking for some empathy and encouragement, and she quickly reminded me that our friend Lisa was having a Tupperware party on Sunday, and I had to go! Believe me when I say going to a Tupperware party was the furthest thing from my mind! She used every trick in the book to get me there, using guilt tactics and then finally bribing me with margaritas. So I finally agreed to go.

That Sunday, I went to the party. I wasn't going to purchase anything because I was just there for support, and margaritas, of course. I had one, two, and then a third margarita, all along listening to this Tupperware lady talk about plastic bowls, cups, microwavable products, and finally the "new" product that would keep your fruits and vegetables fresh in the refrigerator two to three times longer so you don't have to throw out bad produce before you use it. OK. That interested me, but the Tupperware lady didn't interest me at all. I thought she was silly, ditzy, and I was absolutely shocked when she told us she drove a free Tupperware van. My thoughts were racing: "If this lady can earn a free van, maybe I could do the same?" My inner voice was telling me that it was not practical to think I could earn a new minivan for free, so instead of asking more questions about how to earn the van, I decided to challenge the poor gal instead. I questioned her about this new product and came to find out she was actually brilliant. She saw something in me, and she decided to challenge me back. Somehow I had agreed to take her demo product home, slice a tomato into three or four slices, and put one in a baggie, one in whatever container I would normally put a sliced tomato in, and one in her little Tupperware box then hold a Tupperware party on Friday. I had no idea where to put the fourth slice when I got home. The deal was, if the tomato was still fresh in her container that Friday, I would sell Tupperware with her. Game on!

A few days later, she called me to see how many guests I had coming to my party . . . Party? Oh no! I was so busy looking for a job I forgot about the party. Crap! I couldn't look bad in front of her, so I called every friend I knew, telling them this silly story of how she coerced me into having a party and asking if they would please come on Friday evening! Luckily I had good friends, and about twenty of them showed up! I was excited because there were a few items I wanted and thought, "Well, at least I would get some free Tupperware for my family!" Then, low and behold, she reminded me of the challenge. If the tomato was fresh, I would sell Tupperware. The next thing you know, my friends are laughing because that darn tomato was perfectly edible, so that evening I reluctantly became the silly, ditzy Tupperware lady, just like her.

I woke up the next morning thinking, "How could I go from making close to a six-figure income doing what I loved to becoming a Tupperware lady?" So I came up with a plan that I was going to sell plastic bowls until I found a real job to honor my commitment, and then I would quit. I had never been in sales before and had no knowledge of Tupperware products, only that this new little box was a miracle product in my eyes and that the ditzy Tupperware lady had conned me into selling it for her. Then I remembered her saying she had a free van. I decided to tell my husband my plan to sell Tupperware until I found a job, and maybe, just maybe, I could earn a free van in the process, since my lease was almost over on mine. Laughter erupted from him as I told him my idea, and truth be told, that made me furious. I thought, "If that lady could do it, so could I!" Why not? All I had to do is sell a few bowls, right?

Long story short, twelve weeks later, I was not only a manager for Tupperware, I earned a minivan! I was determined to prove to my husband that I could do it. The ditzy manager who had recruited me was actually one of the top earners in the company and was willing to show me how she did it. My self-esteem was rising as well. I loved the recognition I received every time I hit a milestone. After all, there was no one praising me at home for being a wife and mother, and it felt good. Then I realized something along the way. It felt good helping other women (and men), and each time I listened to them about their families, their husbands, losing a job, a new baby, and so on, I wanted to help and shared my story. I believed in each of them, just as my recruiter believed in me. Within months, the activity center was miles behind me, and I was still working around my family's schedule and the money followed. There was just one piece missing. I had labeled myself as "just another ditzy Tupperware lady."

It took about four years into my Tupperware career when I finally changed my mind-set and became proud of what I did. I had just helped my eighth manager earn their Tupperware vehicle, and I cried as he walked across the stage and accepted his recognition. It was at that moment that I realized I had become a top leader in the company in both sales and recruiting. It was never about the plastic bowls to me. It was about the people I met, and the lives that changed, because of my desire to make a difference. I had built a very large team; we celebrated every milestone, we cheered each other on, and we truly believed and encouraged each other. I had learned from the best, and I was able to pass that on to others. I had learned to push myself and push my limits, and I was able to show my children, by example, that you can do anything you set your mind to.

Not only did I earn that first van in three short months, I earned ten Tupperware vans and two cars, including a Saab convertible, in ten years. I earned trips, gifts, and jewelry, as well. I had learned how to talk in front of others, as well as train people to do what I had done. I learned to speak on a stage in front of thousands of people at conventions. My Tupperware career changed my life. It prepared me for many upcoming ventures, including becoming a speaker, an author, a coach, a hypnotherapist, and now the proud owner of Feeling Groovy Wellness, where I teach mind-set first and foremost. Can one bowl change your life? The answer is, yes, it can!

About the Author

Nicole Rhoades is a speaker, author, success coach, vision board coach, master neuro-linguistic programming practitioner, board-certified hypnotherapist, and trainer of both hypnosis and NLP. She is also the founder of Feeling Groovy Wellness, where her mission is to empower others to lead a happy and healthy lifestyle utilizing holistic and natural resources. She believes that a healthy lifestyle begins with making small changes consistently within, finding inner peace and letting go of negative emotions, making healthy food choices, choosing an exercise that you love, surrounding yourself with only positive people, and removing as many toxins as you can from your day-to-day life. Peace, gratitude, and love. You can visit Nicole online at http://www.FeelingGroovyWellness.com.

FROM CODEPENDENCY TO INDEPENDENCY

Scott Transue

When I discover who I am, I'll be free.
Ralph Ellison, *Invisible Man*

Growing up in a home plagued by alcoholism, personal identity was something totally foreign to me. My identity consisted of playing whatever role I needed to on any given day. More often than not, that meant being the one who never got in trouble. My siblings, who were much older than me, had experimented with marijuana and the police were at the house on occasion to speak to them.

What the police never knew about, at least not until much later, was that alcohol abuse was the real culprit. My siblings used marijuana to help deaden the emotional pain. Having no artificial substances to turn to, my only choice was to get through each day as best I could. That almost always meant swallowing my emotions and not even realizing I had needs going unmet.

Dinnertime was always the hardest. My father would have already spent an hour or two at the bar, oftentimes leaving early from work for some extra drinking time. Back then, as long as you got your job done, no one really cared when you left for the day. Knowing that he would end up driving home under the influence, he donated to the police-athletic league regularly, so that they would give him a window sticker. More often than not, if he did get pulled over for erratic driving, he would get a pass because of that window sticker . . . provided he went straight home, of course.

Once home, I never knew whether the night would be quiet or marred by a drunken, out-of-control parent. And, yes, the latter was the rule, rather than the exception. Either dinner was not hot enough or the house wasn't clean enough. Whatever the excuse, it didn't matter. Dad took out his alcohol-fueled anger on Mom. Hour after hour of heated arguing was the norm. All the normal "reasons" applied for why she was the verbal punching bag: If she was a better wife, if she was a better cook, if she kept the house up better . . . Dad wouldn't need to pick a fight.

If that were not enough, I was a skinny, small kid . . . the type all the bigger kids picked on. Loneliness was my lot in life, and I just accepted it. Everybody else was "normal"—everybody else had a "normal" home, with "normal" parents . . . except me. On more than one occasion, I noticed paint cans in the garage. I always had the thought of sniffing enough to require medical attention. After all, you can't ignore a kid in that condition. Maybe, just maybe, someone would notice and actually care. That's all I ever wanted . . . for someone to notice and care.

It all culminated when, as a young teenager, I experienced my first emotional breakdown. My head was telling me to commit suicide, while the logical part of me knew I didn't want to. I was full of fear, anger, and insecurity. I woke Mom up and told her how I was feeling. At this point, my parents had separated . . . sort of. Dad took the upstairs apartment. For God's sake, they couldn't even separate "normally"! She hugged me and told me to grab my sleeping bag so I could "camp out" on the floor of her bedroom: "We'll take care of this in the morning, don't worry." That was enough to quiet my thoughts down.

That episode marked the beginning of a long process of recovery that continues to this day. You might say I actually "discovered" myself. I discovered I was good with numbers, that I was good in front of groups, and that I loved to bowl. I detested the piano lessons my parents "thought" I should be in, but I could spend all day in a bowling center and not lose interest. It was the only sport I could really perform well at, given my slender build. I spent a lot of time in Alateen, a fellowship for children growing up in alcoholic homes. It was the first time I understood that I really was *not* alone. I can say, without hesitation, that Alateen saved my life.

As life progressed, I entered the career world and quickly realized something: I was not a great employee. Not because I couldn't do the work, but because having a "boss" infuriated me. Once again, as in childhood, someone else had the power to determine my future, without a lot of input from me. I "dabbled" in the activities that gave me energy and a sense of self-worth: speaking, doing taxes, and even spending the day at a bowling center. I also joined Toastmasters because there was something about speaking to groups that really jazzed me. I wound up spending over nine years honing my skills, and I am still a member to this day.

At one meeting, a fellow Toastmaster handed me a pamphlet and said, "Didn't you mention one time that you'd love to get paid to speak?" I had indeed, and the pamphlet was for a James Malinchak boot camp. I had never heard of James, but the pamphlet was laid out masterfully.

I attended his multiday "get paid to speak" conference—the light bulb went off. Get paid to do something I had done for free for so many years? What a concept! What I really learned from that conference was that I needed to give myself permission to be me. On a whim, I found a LinkedIn contact who worked for a seminar company. I asked if they needed more speakers, and she said, "Yes!"

I put together a fifteen-minute video of me speaking to an audience and sent it in.

The phone rang twenty-four hours later. My contact wanted to schedule a ninety-minute call with me to discuss the seminar business. We did, and she said she would forward my name to the orientation manager. Orientation manager? Somewhat sheepishly, I will admit, I asked her what the orientation manager would want to discuss. She said, "I thought you said you wanted a speaking contract! I am offering you one, but you need to attend orientation first."

I almost dropped the phone. I would be getting paid to speak, and all I had to do was have the courage to reach out and be me. At around the same time, I found another LinkedIn contact who was writing a book for special-needs families about saving money on their taxes. I had the strangest thought: Why not combine my tax knowledge with my experience as an abuse survivor? I ran the idea past her and she offered me coauthorship. It seems she had contacted multiple CPAs who declined, thinking it wasn't worth their time.

In under a year's time, I had gone from just another "wannabe" speaker to a speaker with a contract and a book in the works. I had also developed friendships with some of the most positive people I had ever met: people who were simply sharing their stories and knowledge—and getting paid *very* well to do it. They continue to inspire me to stretch the comfort zone of what's "possible" for me.

So who am I? I am a speaker and an author. I share my tax knowledge with small-business people. I speak on tax issues, as well as how to get your message out to the world. I represent those with serious illness who need the safety net of disability benefits. I am also an up-and-coming radio show host. I have traveled to twenty-five states giving public seminars and even introduced Eddie Money on stage—and laughed at his rather "colorful" stories of life on the road as a rock star. Regardless of your views on the whole lifestyle, you haven't really lived until you've spent time back-stage with a classic rock star and then introduced him to four hundred people!

Most importantly, I am me . . . and I have learned to embrace that. For me, embracing it means sharing it so others can let that light bulb go off in their heads as it did in mine.

About the Author

Scott Transue is a native of Binghamton, New York, and now resides in Albany, New York. He attended the State University of New York at Albany, earning bachelor's and master's degrees. During his graduate studies, he served as a graduate fellow on the New York State Assembly Ways and Means Committee.

Scott is a member of Toastmasters, earning Advanced Communicator Bronze and Advanced Leader Bronze designations.

He is the president of Scott Transue International LLC, a speaking and training firm. He is also the owner of Freedom Day Tax and Accounting LLC.

He delivers training seminars regularly for National Seminars and Compliance Online. You can contact Scott by phone at 518-210-1419, on his website www.ScottTransue.com, or by email at stransue01@gmail.com.

GETTING BACK
IN THE GAME

---

*From Bullied to Bold: Discovering One's
True Identity through Self-Empowerment*

Dr. Deborah Hrivnak

Don't let your struggle become your identity.

Ralston Bowles

He never wanted to play football but was forced into the role of kicker. However, because of his well-trained soccer skills, he nailed a fifty-yard field goal in his first high school game. With this great start, here is our hero, standing on the sidelines, waiting to see if he'll be "back in the game."

Have you ever been totally prepared for one thing, then thrust into another, and yet your work ethic and abilities got you to the proverbial corner office only to be sidelined? If so, the kicker's story, your story, and my story, are much the same.

One might ask, "Who am I"? My identity was that of a success and now this?!?! Can this possibly end well? Read on to find out how the kicker's story ends, how my story is related, and how yours might end.

Growing up as a young child, my family taught me the benefits of a strong work ethic, responsibility, integrity, and the ability to get along well with others. I became as physically tough as I was mentally tough working on my grandparent's farm. My fondest memories are the incessant teasing I experienced, especially from my uncles. This was a commonplace activity when I was with my family, and I recognized early on that it was a mode of play and vital to my self-identity. It taught me a way of creating bonds, showing affection, and dealing with conflict. I could laugh at myself and not take things too seriously. Bullying was not in my experience.

Just as our hero in the picture was prepared to be a soccer star, I was prepared and encouraged to go to college, never aspiring to become a teacher, yet the admiration and inspiration I felt for a family member at a very young age led me to become a special educator and then, administrator. I was inspired by her work that sounded unique and different from any vocation to which I had been exposed. My sophomore year of college, I made the decision to go into special education so that I, too, might make a difference in the lives of others.

Working in special education suited me well. Despite the high burnout rate among teachers, I thrived. One cannot burn out when walking the soybean fields—one learns to keep moving ahead one step after another. My skill set provided me with the tools I needed to become very successful in a highly rewarding career. I loved the variety and complexity of working with disabled students. I worked with outstanding administrators, as well as supportive staff and parents. Collaborating and being highly organized and responsible allowed me to juggle the complexities and chaos that one might otherwise experience in special education. In addition to classroom instruction, I loved scheduling and facilitating meetings, conducting assessments, completing paperwork, scheduling, working with budgets, training and supervising paraprofessionals, and data collection.

My identity as a successful professional in the arena of special education—as teacher, administrator, and professor—was firmly established. None of this prepared me for events and encounters that would cause me to lose sight of my identity as a success.

With numerous life transitions and many challenges, I learned I was strong, resilient, and able to survive, despite my circumstances. I always bounced back, appreciated the support of family and friends, and continued to enjoy my work. Stress is an inevitable part of life and the stress I experienced along the journey provided the motivation I needed to meet any challenge.

Thirty years into my career, my sons had grown up to be fine and outstanding young men. Both had married and were happy in their work. I was blessed to have been in a wonderful relationship with a man I loved for seven years, and I worked as an administrator in one of the best school districts in the nation. Life was good! Within a year, John was offered a lucrative position with a company, and if I wanted to continue with our relationship, it would require me to resign from my job, leave my family and friends, and relocate to another state. I was very excited about my "new" life with John, the financial opportunities this move would provide us, and the excitement of growing the life-coaching business I had created starting in 2004, playing in a larger arena and greater opportunities.

> *There are some things you learn best*
> *in calm, and some in storm.*
> **Willa Cather, *The Song of the Lark***

Our storm had just begun. Immediately following the excitement of moving and being together, having financial stability, and renovating a home that was ours, the economic conditions in our country brought job loss for John within six months of our move. I was finding it more and more difficult to get not only a job offer but even an interview, and we were now living in our dream home in the midst of renovation. My dream for growing my coaching business changed rapidly with the need for a job just to pay the bills. What happened? Where did I lose my identity, my success, and all that came with it?

Back in the game within a couple of months, I was offered a job in special education administration with phenomenal pay. This would allow us to keep our home, and I was not disappointed with the chance to demonstrate my leadership skills and take on more responsibility. In addition, I had the opportunity to fulfill a lifelong dream of completing my doctorate in educational leadership. Life, then, threw another curve ball in the form of a job loss due to restructuring. I was back on the sidelines!

Job loss can be devastating—it can also be a blessing. I was also grateful to be getting out of this position. The stress was more than I had ever experienced before. I was anxious for a new and better opportunity. For the first time in my life, I had begun to question who I was, and I recognized my confidence in myself, and my work had plummeted. Any success as an educator or life coach seemed to have faded away. My next job offer provided the financial security I needed, and it would also provide me with a level of success I had never experienced before . . . through struggle.

Within the first week on that job, a colleague shared her experience of harassment and bullying during her first year. I didn't heed her warning for "new people," as I knew nothing like that could possibly happen to me. I learned that bullying is, unfortunately, not all that rare. The Workplace Bullying Institute in 2014 reported that sixty-five million individuals are affected by workplace bullying, and for two more years, I was one of those statistics. I experienced the following:

- Tampering with my professional files and records
- Belittling my professional decisions
- Constantly criticizing my work
- Yelling and profanity
- Intimidation
- Impeding my work by withholding documents
- Constantly changing my work expectations
- Assigning an unreasonable work load and establishing impossible deadlines

As a result, I experienced shock, anger, feelings of frustration and helplessness, depression, and anxiety. I could not sleep and experienced ongoing panic attacks. I felt an overwhelming sense of injustice. How could this have happened to me? Why had my employer (human resources, assistant superintendent, administrators association) inadequately responded to my formal complaints, and why were friends and colleagues willing to stand on the sidelines? Long-term effects included the diagnosis of type 2 diabetes, lingering feelings of anger, difficulty trusting people, reduced occupational opportunities, and significant challenges recognizing who I was and who I had become.

Certainly job loss setbacks—being sidelined—would never happen again, or so I thought. I was fortunate to spend my third year in a new and different position with an outstanding supervisor. I had positive experiences and received distinguished evaluations throughout the year. My "less than adequate" evaluations were erased from the system, and I felt that somehow, someone actually knew and understood what had happened to me in previous years.

Then it happened again. I was certain I would experience another "restructuring" for the third time, and I did. To this day, I cannot answer why any of this happened, especially in a career I enjoyed for decades. Although another job loss brought me to my knees, I would not allow it to keep me sidelined for good.

Life doesn't give us do-overs, and yet we can learn from our experiences. Here are a few of the lessons I learned:

- Life is unfair . . . keep moving forward.
- Be grateful for what is.
- We get to choose who it is we want to be, and how we show up.
- Take care of yourself.
- Surround yourself with people who support you and what you do.
- Learn to forgive others.

- Get back in touch with your faith, and be who it is God created you to be.

What of our hero? This soccer player, forced to kick a football, ended up playing for the National Champion Nebraska Huskers, establishing records in indoor football, and was recruited by the 49ers. He's now living in Lincoln, Nebraska, with his wife and three children. That is "in the game."

I set out to pursue my dream of public speaking and success coaching. I immersed myself in various programs to learn everything needed to have a successful business. I joined a mastermind program and released toxic individuals from my life. I took better care of myself. I wrote a book, *Get off the Sidelines and into the "Game": Quotes to Inspire a Game Plan for Successful Living*. Using a strengths-based philosophy, I show others how to get into the "game" and create a game plan that maximizes their potential.

There are going to be times in our lives that we do not understand. We will be uncomfortable and may not know where to turn, what to do, or where to go. When we are disempowered and lose our identity through life circumstances, we have the choice to engage and empower ourselves.

We can lose sight of who we are, but we never truly lose our true identity. You can reconnect and become "more than you can ask or imagine, according to his power that is at work within us." Ephesians 3:20.

About the Author

Dr. Deborah J. Hrivnak is a professional speaker, coach, author, and the creator of the Four-Step Game Plan for How to Take Action and Get off the Sidelines and into the "Game." She is the president and CEO of MyCoachDeborah, Inc., where she integrates her strengths-based philosophy, action-oriented approach, candor, and humor to support individuals toward greater success in their lives. Before starting her own business, Deborah served as a special education teacher and administrator, as well as a university professor. Her book, *Get off the Sidelines and into the "Game,"* can be found on Amazon, and Deborah can be reached at http://www.MyCoachDeborah.com.

WHEN IDENTITY CHOOSES YOU

Deana Petrelli

What lies behind us and what lies ahead of us are tiny matters compared to what lives within us.

Henry David Thoreau

Discovering your identity . . . what a novel idea. But what happens when identity chooses you instead?

As far back as I can remember, I was a trendsetter, refusing to accept the norm in just about everything. I was always looking for new and creative ways to express myself. This included giving myself and my Barbie awesome random haircuts behind my mom's favorite couch. Oh, if you could only see the amazing work I did with a pair of dull scissors and no mirror! My mother was always impressed with my creativity . . . Not! She kindly called me an "active child." I did not like watching television and constantly had to be discovering things to keep myself occupied. I remember dressing up my dogs in makeshift outfits to put on "plays" for my family. I loved to act and entertain, especially when it shocked the norm.

I'd blow up science projects in our basement or dive into the local creek to investigate the nature that lived inside the waters. I hated being told what I should and should not like or what I was supposed to act like because I was a girl. I remember wanting a boys' BMX bike because I hated the look of the banana seat on the girls' bikes. I negotiated like a pro for everything I wanted—so much so that my family called me the "little attorney."

At age five, I pretended I was a news anchor with my best friend. With a tape recorder, we would recount our days with silly bits of information, like who picked their nose, what movie we saw, or what kind of shenanigans we had gotten into. My first experience with supply, demand, and people's buying preferences came from a lesson I learned on the school bus one day. At the age of six, I was eating a small piece of candy when other kids began asking me for some. Being stingy, I didn't want to share, so I said, "Sure, but it will cost you," and named an outrageous price. Suddenly, kids were digging in their pockets, backpacks, and shoving each other to hold out cash. This raised the price into a straight-out, cold bidding war. That day, a light bulb came on inside my head, and the entrepreneur in me was unleashed.

Thereafter, I began to test different products or services to see if they stood up to their claims. I also wanted to see if they were worth what they cost. I would have my parents take me to events or the store to buy products or sample services. I would try them out and give my opinion in the form of a review. I always tried to find cheaper alternatives that could perform the same as, or better than, their expensive counterparts. I became totally fascinated with the idea of supply, demand, and the reasons behind people's buying preferences. I learned to test the market on consumers with products, services, and their price points. I quickly discovered that often what sells is mostly what people want or like, which tends to be much different than what they need.

In high school, my passion continued. I immersed myself into fashion, hair, makeup, and sports. I dyed my hair blonde, red, purple, blue, and once a bad product dyed my hair green by accident! I would get frustrated if I couldn't find a product that had the fashion, style, or color I wanted. I even taught myself to sew, turning my visions into outfits. I became well known as an information hub for products, services, or entertainment. My friends and family constantly asked my opinion on a variety of things. I was always more than happy to oblige.

At sixteen years old, I became a dog trainer/handler, working with akitas in American Kennel Club dog shows. My personal dog weighed more than me and always pranced around the ring with the confidence of a king. Showing dogs was an expensive endeavor. To cut costs, my dad and I were always looking for ways to let my dog stand out without spending a fortune. Most of the breeders used a special dog shampoo that was $150, a $300 dryer, and exotic food supplements. As you can guess, I refused to conform to the norm. My dog was not kenneled, and to keep him looking amazing, I did what I had always done and started to experiment with different products and services. I knew I could achieve the same results for less money. I did it with a great bargain brand of shampoo and conditioner for people! My dog had the softest, brightest, and shiniest coat in the ring. He consistently won first place in nearly every show he was ever entered in. My dad would tell the breeders some elaborate nonsense when they would ask what we were using. We would laugh the whole way home. This product discovery we kept as our winning secret!

A few years later, I was competing in a beauty pageant. I didn't want to spend a lot of money for a one-night event, so I began my hunt for quality products and services. I used my prom dress for the formal competition, vintage jewelry from my grandmother, and did my hair and makeup with quality drugstore brands. What do you know? It felt good to be crowned! I spent a year representing my city as queen. I was even recruited to be a model representative for a popular and well-known beer company. Due to being at so many events, chamber mixers, grand openings, and so on,

I eventually included more entertainment, events, venues, music, and television into my reviews.

During that time, I also went to college and chose to go into a career that was primarily male dominated. I was bucking the norm again. During my eleven successful years in this field, I was used as a model in print ads and recruiting to attract women into this career field. I have always been outgoing, talkative, and consistently on the hunt for new things. I take pride in being on the cutting edge of everything before everyone else!

When I bought my first property, I got interested in real estate. As a hobby, I explored design, remodeling, construction, home staging, buying, and selling. I had to trendset or I wasn't happy. In four years, I sold my first property for double what I originally paid for it. My research and testing of products and services had paid off big time, scoring me a handsome profit.

I eventually became a wife and a stay-at-home mom. Having more time on my hands, and loving to continue to learn, I also became an avid reader. This led me to posting book reviews about my most recent finds. As parenthood became part of life, I began exploring new products for kids and families.

As the years ticked by, my friends and family continued to come to me for my opinions. This advanced to friends of friends as well. Eventually, my husband became annoyed at the fact that strangers would constantly stop us wherever we were at to ask about my makeup, hair, outfit, or some new product I was using. He told me to start putting the information into a blog or videos so I could just refer people to my site for resources instead of spending time explaining it to them at dinner, the beach, and so on.

I guess I never put much thought into the word identity . . . that is until my identity chose me. *Petrelli Reviews* was always inside me trying to reveal itself. Now it's finally official. As always, I'm your one-stop lifestyle resource on what's hot, what's not, and everything in between in the world of products, services, and entertainment reviews.

About the Author

Deana Petrelli is the CEO and founder of Petrelli Reviews. She is a radio-show host, hard-core consumer, blogger, book author, and former beauty queen. She is a leading expert in professional product, service, and entertainment reviews.

If you want to know what's trending, what's worth your hard-earned cash, what's a waste of money, and all that middle ground in-between, check out her lifestyle blog at PetrelliReviews .com. You can also join her weekly for her radio show on RockStarWorldwide.com, where she discusses all your favorite topics, mixing it up each week with professional product, service, and entertainment reviews for the people.

DO WHAT YOU CAN, WHERE YOU ARE, WITH WHAT YOU HAVE

Fran Jessee

*Do what you can, with what you
have, where you are.*

Theodore Roosevelt

How much do I love entrepreneurs? Let me count the ways . . .

Rome wasn't built in a day . . . and neither did I learn in a day, as I am many days old! I treasure everything I've been through in my life because it's made me a person I care about today. I didn't always care about myself. That took many, many life lessons and revelations.

I was born in Glendale, California . . . from the wrong side of the tracks, as they say. I always wanted to be like the "popular girls" because they had "things." Being on the poorer side, I always thought making money would make me happy. It took about nineteen years past being a teenager to realize that was not the quest I needed to pay attention to.

For all intents and purposes, before I was thirty-six years old, I had some wonderful things take place and a few dramatic upsets. I found the love of my life, married at nineteen, and had two beautiful kids, a son and a daughter. Perfect! Then sadly, as so many, I was divorced at twenty-seven. Simultaneously, I found myself starting my first business in 1971, FJ Graphics, a typesetting and graphics firm, back in the days when they still cut and pasted with X-Acto knives. I even knew how to use a darkroom for photography. I was always an excellent typist and very ambitious. Thus began a lifelong journey into a professional career in the printing industry, leading to sales, advertising, promotion, publishing, marketing, and eventually entrepreneurship! Being an entrepreneur is the most amazing journey in my life . . . besides having my beautiful kids and my cats. Money is always important but not the main goal, or I would have been "rich" by now.

Since the early 1980s, I've indulged in many self-help books and learned from favorite authors, spiritual leaders, and ministers. Around this time, I received an awakening, which changed the pursuit of money making me happy to learning more about the pursuit of being a more spiritual person and putting my trust in God. I still love my classic tools. Here are a few that

I remember that made big impacts in my life . . . and still do:

- Alcoholics Anonymous' Twelve-Step Program
- Norman Vincent Peale, weekly sermons with a great sense of humor
- Dr. Robert Schuller, *Hour of Power*, Crystal Cathedral
- Joyce Meyer, Daily Sermons
- Napoleon Hill, *Think and Grow Rich*
- U. S. Anderson, *Three Magic Words*
- George S. Clason, *The Richest Man in Babylon*
- Raam Daas, *The Only Dance There Is*
- Wayne Dyer, many, many lectures and books

There are so many—too many to mention. And I love phrases with a meaning in a nutshell, simplifying a long philosophical meaning.

For me, entrepreneurship involves cultivating an idea from scratch. I've never been able to get as enthused about "selling other people's products and ideas" as much as I have my own creations. However, that's where I was able to make my living, for the most part.

In the early 1990s, I launched my first "idea." They were called "Candy Cards"—a small bag of color-coordinated Jelly Belly candies (very popular at the time because President Reagan ate them every day). This idea came to me in 1988 when I wanted to give my customer something different for St. Patrick's Day. I printed some little header cards with a leprechaun image on them, bagged up some Green Apple Jelly Bellys, and gave them as a calling card. They were very well received, leading me into designing and launching a whole line of Candy Cards with different greetings, such as "Happy Birthday," "You're Special," "Get Well," and so on. On the back, I printed "To" and "From" and had them in lots and lots of gift and flower shops. I had to let that business go because I could not get funding, it was not patentable, and it was just too hard to keep it going. I went back to the real world of a "job" in publishing books and so on.

In 1997 for Christmas, I made a painting in acrylic colors for nine of my friends and family in which I painted a heart theme using the "Love Is Patient, Love Is Kind" phrases under different colors of hearts. When I finished making all those originals, I knew someday I wanted to see that design on items like journals, tote bags, mugs, and t-shirts. I was currently in a group of women studying the book called *The Artists Way*, written by Julia Cameron, which also changed my life into understanding that I had my own creative nature inside me. In 2001, I made that dream a reality by launching a website called "A Giftful Heart" (http://www.agiftfulheart.com). In 2005, my daughter took it over, and the designs were changed from "Love Is Patient" to "Save the Date" for the wedding industry. It is still thriving today. I went back to work to help her in 2006 and stayed until February 2015, only to take a leave to start my current startup Longevity Spice Blends: Organic Spices for Better Health.

While working for my daughter at A Giftful Heart, another idea was sparked from my chiropractor. One Saturday, in April 2010, I set out to Spic 'n Span and kind of reorganize my apartment. I cleaned in, under, and around everything, from about 7:30 pm to about 4:00 pm. I sat down and couldn't get back up. Oh dear! What do I do now?! For three more days, it was quite agonizing . . . then it subsided enough so I could get around again. I knew I didn't want to live my life not being able to do anything physical. In my research, I came across Dr. Ron Bittle of Peak Performance Chiropractic. I began regular adjustments over four years ago, became a believer in chiropractic medicine, and learned why it is so beneficial to me. I began helping him by doing graphics for his coupons over many months. I accumulated so many different designs that I decided to offer them to other chiropractors; hence, "ChiroCoupons" came to life. I just love the process of starting a new business. In fact, that's what I'm best at—developing all the parts and pieces that go into it. Once I get them up and running, then the real work comes in. Getting the business, doing the work and "management," that's about where I get bored with it. I knew I wasn't going to quit my "day job." It was very labor intensive, and soon I decided I didn't want to work that hard. This little business wouldn't really offer me the kind of income that would have been worth the effort. While building it, I'm challenged, up earlier than the birds, making things happen!

Next—another favorite—my fun, beautiful, wonderful, colorful Design-a-Kitty was born! Earlier in the decade, around 2000, my daughter had bought me a little stuffed, beaded kitty at the Montrose Arts and Crafts Festival. We both loved it so much, but I just knew I wanted to make my own someday and also sell them at craft fairs. So it sat on my shelf for years . . . being admired. And then, a year or so after putting ChiroCoupons on the shelf, I must have been a bit bored again, because I looked at it and said, "Let's just do this now."

It seems most of my ideas have incubated for periods of time, and then I can't stop myself. They just have to come to life! So I set out looking for fabrics and beads and any kind of jewelry that might be suitable for my new stuffed kitties at garage sales and so on and accumulated a houseful of materials in a short amount of time. I designed a template, bought a beautiful, older, "mechanical" Kenmore sewing machine on Craigslist, and drove all the way from Valencia to Palmdale to pick it up, for $25! I still have that stuck away, and it works like a charm. Not sure when I'll ever use it again, but some things have a bit of meaning to me. I made lots and lots of kitties. The kids *loved* them, but the moms said they cost too much ($32), and my other part of this story—of being able to design their kitties online—didn't come to life either: again . . . lack of funds (or not meant to be . . . whichever fits, it's hard to figure that out).

So now what do I do with all that fabric, beads, and jewelry? No brainer . . . learn to make jewelry! Oh dear! I didn't see that one coming! My passion grew deeper and deeper, as I was mesmerized by all the beads, stones, meanings, colors, options, which I still *love* to work with today.

Currently in 2015, my newest venture and, I think, most purposeful idea is . . . I have developed a brand new organic spice blend called Longevity Spice Blends: Organic Spice Blends for Better Health. From my own personal desire to live, not just a long life, but more important, a healthy life, I have created five different blends: twenty-four Full of Life Spices and Herbs with antiaging and anti-inflammatory benefits, twenty-four beautiful spices for brain boosting, nineteen awesome spices for detox now, fourteen healthy spices for digestion and acid reflux, and twenty-two spices for the common cold, flu, and congestion. I have many more to add.

About the Author

Fran Jessee graduated from many schools, and they all graciously awarded her certificates from the School of Hard Knocks. She was born a self-actualized entrepreneur, but that wasn't uncovered until around forty-five years into her life.

Born in Glendale, California, in the 1940s, she had the awesome experience of living her teenage years in the 1950s, when there were streetcars to downtown LA, there were cruise nights on Brand Blvd., and Bob's Big Boy was the place to go! There were t-strap and white buck saddle shoes, and boyfriends and girlfriends were top priority. There were even bumper-to-bumper cruise nights on Hollywood Blvd. with seltzer bottles and egg throwing. She was ambitious very early and a quick learner on her jobs, leading her to start her first business in her twenties in the fields of typesetting and graphics and the world of print and advertising. Being around creativity opened doors to help her realize her own creativity, which led her to be the true entrepreneur she is today.

Her current passions include the following:

- *Longevity Spice Blends for Better Health.* She has developed and blended her own healthy, organic line of spices for specific health issues, such as inflammation, detox, brain health, digestion, congestion, and so on. Find more information at http://www.longevityspiceblends.com.
- *Jewelry design.* See her work online at http://www.etsy.com/shop/inspiration101.

IT'S NOT WHAT YOU DO

Kathy Pendleton

*Human identity is the most fragile thing we have,
and it's often only found in moments of truth.*

Alan Rudolph

Who am I? Who are you? Have these questions ever puzzled you? They certainly have puzzled me. What criteria should I use to determine the answer? Is it what I do? Maybe, but that changes. Is it my name? Perhaps, but that changed, too. My occupation or profession? More changes. Over the years, I've learned about myself—that I've missed the passion that others have for their life's work. It's been missing for me, and I keep wondering why I don't feel that way. The realization of what I feel consistently has come gradually. Over time, I've observed my behavior, working to discover my feelings.

It was a beautiful, sunny summer day when I was six years old. There was a younger boy who lived down the street and always seemed to get picked on. It made me mad. On that day, I heard him yelling and I took off to take care of him and save him from the kids who were messing with him. We were all little kids then, and it wasn't a big deal. I did the same thing in high school for a fellow student. We were in a trigonometry class together, and she just didn't get it. I really liked the teacher and the subject, but I didn't like that he picked on students occasionally. One day, he started picking on my friend, and I retaliated with words. It was uncomfortable! But I realized that I retaliated when the underdog got picked on. I still don't like it and often still retaliate, more on behalf of others than for myself. This trait, I believe, is part of my identity. I'm still learning to use it responsibly.

In my early teens, I wanted to be a doctor to help people. I was told that it would be silly to invest all that time and money in an education that I'd never use. My destiny was to become a wife and mother, find a husband who'd want to support me and our family, and then devote my attention to raising our children. I didn't become a doctor, but I also didn't become a wife and mother. I took a different path.

While a teenager, my high school offered an exchange-student program. The organization we worked with managed exchanges with countries in South America. I was determined to be chosen! In spite of the fact that I studied French in high school, I was chosen and

I traveled to Peru. My family spoke as much English as I spoke Spanish. I was immersed in the challenge of learning to communicate with my adopted family. The adventure unfolded! It was my first time on a plane, my first time in another country, my first time eating four meals a day and dinner at 9:00 p.m. There were so many firsts. And I discovered that I loved travel. I still do. This is another part of my identity.

Near the end of high school, I began applying to colleges. I had never even considered the possibility of another option. My two best friends had no desire whatsoever to go to college, and I was astounded by that. We three took very different paths for a number of years before reuniting as adults with similar interests—finding jobs, making an income, and deciding how we would live our lives. The acceptance of the fluidity of friendship, and knowing that it can still be strong in spite of distance and time, is definitely a part of my identity.

In college, I encountered my first real failure. After transferring to an out-of-state university for my second year, my grades went from a 3.8 GPA as a freshman to getting a 1.7 GPA that first term away from home. My successful student identity was built around getting good grades, so I felt like a complete failure. I learned that some mistakes hang on and impact your future— that is, it would be very difficult to bring that poor GPA up to an honors level before graduation. These experiences contributed, very painfully, to my early sense of independence, to my sense that "you get by with a little help from your friends," and to my analysis of what really mattered to me.

After graduation, I had to find a job without having a clear vision of what I wanted to do. I had gotten a minor in education but had also discovered that teaching junior and senior high school was not for me—another contribution to my identity, I suppose. Thanks to the many computer software classes I had taken, somewhat new at the time, the opportunity arose to work in software development for a computer manufacturer and to move to Florida, all on my own. I signed on the dotted line.

It turned out to be the most difficult year of my life! The company was small, and my department consisted of fourteen of the most conservative men I had ever met. I was completely on my own, a zillion miles from home and friends, and all long-distance calls were charged by the minute. I longed to have a close friend, longed to have a boyfriend, longed for an easy familiarity with the people around me. It took a long time for those things to develop. Here's what I discovered: I don't enjoy cooking a nice meal only for myself. I really dislike heat and working on a tan. I love unique areas of the world, like the Everglades and the Florida Keys. And I did *not* like working in software development!

It took three years to get out of there! During the third year, my role shifted to primarily customer support for two reasons: I loved it and was good at it. The education degree paid off! I loved, and still do, figuring out how to explain complex concepts and organize course material. I love mastering technical information and still do. I still love travel! Within a short time, I was traveling to teach classes to customers. I love meeting new people, and I'm very good at remembering names. I love seeing the light bulb go on when I've successfully explained a very complicated concept or process. These traits are part of my identity.

So my life was shaping up. Warm and familiar high school relationships had been rekindled. I'd discovered some things about life and work that I loved and also some things that I didn't. But what about a love relationship? Here's what I had discovered about that: I fell in love too fast. Luckily my boyfriends had been very nice, but I didn't have a vision of what I wanted or how to evaluate whether I was getting it. In reality, I moved from long-term relationship to long-term relationship, and it seemed that the next guy was strong in the deficiencies of the previous guy. Have you experienced that? Breakups were slow and painful. One thing I did notice was that I often dreamed about being a bird in a cage and I wasn't interested in babies. How could this eventually work, with the predicted role of wife and stay-at-home mom? What piece of my identity would be filled in from these characteristics?

After many years, I repeated the completely independent move experience, this time to Germany. It was a much better experience the second time around. I made friends faster, learned to be alone more easily, and fulfilled a longtime dream of living and working outside the United States. Friends and family came to visit, and I thoroughly enjoyed the role of tour guide. The adventure lasted two and a half years, and a large part of the enjoyment was joining the "ex-patriot club." Living in a different country is so different than vacationing there. Meeting the challenges of a different language, different customs, different food . . . so many differences made it exciting and exhilarating to me. I truly believe that observing and adapting is a very deep and treasured part of my identity.

When I returned to the United States, it was to the headquarters of the company, located in the heart of Silicon Valley in California. It was familiar and a pleasure to be back in the United States. I already had many friends because of the numerous business trips there over the years that I worked for the company. Despite my excitement for exploring, I love the feeling of relaxing into a familiar environment. That feeling truly begins when I run into someone I know out and about in town.

I met and began dating the man I would marry. With him, I never dreamed about the caged bird. We're both very independent, and that enables us to each continue what we love to do, separately from one another. We also enjoy traveling together and going to the theatre, symphony, and sporting events together. It's been a fun and busy life for the past twenty-five years.

I left my corporate career in 2000 and was looking for something new to pursue, but that question of "What are you passionate about?" haunted me. I wasn't really passionate about anything. I liked things, but there was nothing that I couldn't live without. I joined the Junior League and spent many seasons with Team in Training. I loved the feeling of contributing in my community and making a difference in peoples' lives. Still, it didn't provide the passion that I was seeking. I started entrepreneurial ventures, which interested me only in their ability to make money. Without the necessary passion, they were soon abandoned, money making or not. Would I ever find an interest that would generate the passion that others talked about?

During these years, my family members were suffering from health issues. I often found myself in the hospital, lending my support during medical procedures. Ever the observer, and always interested in the medical profession and industry, I realized that I held a vision for how I expected medical treatment to work. In the early 1980s, I had spent many hours discussing health care with an RN who owned a home health agency. I hadn't understood to what level I had internalized those discussions. When pain medication wasn't ordered post-surgery for my mother-in-law, leaving her in excruciating pain, I became furious. After showing my temper to the nurses, I was still unable to make any difference. My discomfort at my ineffectiveness lasted many minutes while my mother-in-law suffered. I was equally uncomfortable about how I might be able to help her. Finally, I touched her and whispered a guided meditation to help her release the pain and tension. My father-in-law was amazed as she relaxed, stopped moaning, and dropped off to sleep. I was amazed, too . . . and grateful . . . very, very grateful.

There were other similar occurrences. Through situations like these, I realized how much they include parts of my identity that I treasure. As patients, we must sign our acceptance of medical treatments we often don't understand, receive the treatment in facilities whose organization and functioning we don't understand, and play by rules that are rarely explained. How patients can participate in their treatment involves understanding, observation, and uncommon assertiveness. What parts of my identity are stirred by these challenges—complexity, analysis, possibly teaching and travel, making a real difference in the lives of others. I can feel my passion rising to the challenge, and I'm working in this area now.

I don't know how others search for and find their identities. For me, it's been a slow process of getting to know myself, and the journey isn't over yet. I encourage you to take on a similar journey of your own. It's worth all the effort.

About the Author

Kathy Pendleton grew up in Virginia, toward the end of the era of life-long careers and marriages and stay-at-home moms. The product of an idyllic childhood in a neighborhood of many children, jump rope, and hide-and-seek, she was expected to lead a life similar to that of her parents. Can you relate to that?

After college, Kathy embarked on a twenty-six-year career in the computer industry, mostly in technical education and customer support, roles in which she excelled. Her strengths in analyzing, simplifying, and teaching complex computer processes led her to fulfill dreams of travel, living outside the USA, and appreciation for many varying points of view.

Since leaving the computer industry, Kathy continues to travel and expand her horizons through a wide variety of interests, including theatre, medical advocacy, personal growth, and entrepreneurship. She and her husband, Tom, live near Lake Tahoe.

FINDING IDENTITY IN PASSION

Carol Shockley

I realize then that it's not enough to know what someone is called. You have to know who they are.

Gayle Forman, *Just One Day*

When I thought of writing a story on identity, I thought, "What do I know on this topic?" As I pondered, and I heard others speak on identity, I began to realize we each have a few different identities throughout life. Now I have a few stories I could share on this topic, easily. I could write about my identity as a mother, as the baby of the family, as a woman, as an event planner, or as me, overall. Each of these different identities makes me who I am today.

Each of our identities begins with where we have been, and who we've become, as an individual.

Finding Identity in Passion

Who the world views us as is not as
important as how we see ourselves.

Carol Shockley

My identity started when I was a child, when everyone would call me "Daddy's Girl." When in reality,
I wanted and desired to be "Mommy's Girl." I never
had that down home mother-daughter relationship—
the one where you cooked in the kitchen with mom,
did crafts with your mom, or enjoyed heart-to-heart
talks with your mom throughout junior high and high
school. I was solo and had my friends to lean on . . . then
boys. What happened next was becoming a mom at
age eighteen to my first daughter. At this point, my life
shifted, as did my identity.

My identity became "mom." At eighteen, I was what
many referred to as "a baby having a baby." My little girl
became my world. Everything I knew I was going to do
was to provide for her and be there for her in every way I
knew how to be. I continued having children until I was
twenty-three, and I decided no more. The three children
I had were my life, and everything they needed, I was
going to provide for them: from their emotional needs,
their educational needs, and playing sports. Growing up
with my kids was one of the hardest, and greatest, joys
in my life. There were times I wondered what life would
have been like if I had had them later in my years and how
much more I could of given and taught them. That was

until I shared those thoughts with my youngest, and she said, "Mom, I wouldn't change anything with you. My friends never had the opportunity to watch their moms grow and become who they are because they waited. With you, mom, I've watched you grow, I've watched you struggle, I've watched you overcome, and I get to watch you go after your dreams and succeed."

Since my youngest has graduated, I have entered into a new phase of my life—again, a new identity.

My identity now is evolving, just like the ones before have done, too. Who am I now, as I go into this new phase in my life? Sometimes I still ask myself this question in the morning. I am still a daughter; I am still a mother; and I am now an event planner. How did I become an event planner? In the past few years, I've asked myself that question a number of times. Our life experiences all add up and give us clues as to our gifts, our talents, and our skills. First, I could tell you that while I was a child, I loved to collect items and go home, set up an event, invite friends over, and educate them on a topic—kind of like school. As a teenager, I loved being a part of community activities, basketball, color guard, and jazz band and being a part of planning youth activities, summer camp, and organizations. The administration process always excited me. Most of the jobs I held were in the IT field and client support. I enjoyed coordinating the teams that supported the clients and educating teams on new software programs.

The more consulting I did, the less contact I had with consumers, which led me to realize that I thrived on the interaction of people. I decided to change industries and go back to school. I wanted to understand groups of people. I studied social science for my associate's degree and continued onto sociology for my bachelor's degree. Once I completed those, I wanted to know more, so I went for my MBA and specialized in marketing. I loved school and wasn't sure how any of this education was going to help me.

During school, I held a job coordinating forty-eight classrooms throughout each weekend, which required the dedication of a team of volunteers. I now found myself as a leader and a team coordinator of volunteers. This is where I learned about relationships on a deeper level. I was just me; an individual loving other individuals, helping them find a place of involvement and where they could find fulfillment in making the difference in a child's life. I had thought I found my niche. I found everything that made me tick on the inside. I had to be organized, I had to tackle administrative tasks, I had to juggle a diversity of tasks at any given moment, and I had to build relationships. All these things come naturally for me, and I was in my element.

One day, it had to end, and we relocated. What did I do from there? I went back to organizing a team around the globe for a software merger, still using my strengths and skills. We moved once again, and this time without my husband, as he deployed overseas. I was still in the identity of being "Mom," so I decided to stay home and be "Mom" without a dad in the home. It just so happens that the right opportunity always shows up, and I got a position as a personal assistant (PA) to a corporate entertainer and speaker. During my time as a PA, we traveled to large events, and I ran the back of the room sales—a new area that I thrived in and enjoyed. Also, we put a show on the Vegas strip for six months—from scheduling, to box office, to promotions, sales, and show times with guest appearances. Each opportunity expands our experiences for our journey.

The time I spent working as a PA, I started learning more about the speaking industry and events. It was now that it was going to start to come together. I met another speaker in which one of the first conversations I had with him a year prior was with the intuition of knowing I was going to work with him one day, but I had no idea how. Sure enough, one and a half years later, he was having a struggle finding the right event planner to assist with his events. I had reached out and asked if I could help with one event while he continued to search. His response was "Yes!" I had no idea of the details of managing an event. I just knew the knowledge I had from the show on the strip, from the back of the room sales, and from working as a PA that I could do it. I knew how important it was for him to be able to do "his thing" from stage. I was up for it, and he believed in me.

Oh my goodness! That week in March 2012 changed my identity. I fell in love! I had never been more alive than from the moment I stepped into my natural element that first week. Work had always been work, not fully draining though. I wasn't alive like I had been, executing and pulling the strings for such a large event of three hundred people and four days of continuous activity. Needless to say, I didn't crash of exhaustion until twenty-four hours after the tear-down of the event. I had found my purpose, my passion—you know? That one thing that wakes you up in the morning . . . I found it at that time.

My identity has been evolving since that day, understanding what it takes to be an event planner and an entrepreneur. You have to understand your "why"—the reason you want to do what you do.

I froze six months in and didn't fully wake up again as myself, with my own identity, for a year later. It finally all clicked within me. But how? It was when I allowed myself to trust myself—when I decided that I could do things my way. Yes, there is common sense; yes, others have opinions; and yes, I could filter the advice I was receiving from those in my circle.

I had to learn, for myself, that my intuition knows best, for me. I had to understand that no one has the perfect answer or advice and that I could trust myself, above all. I have reached a place in business where I have enjoyed opportunities I would have never thought possible. I have relationships with individuals that I would have never thought possible. I have traveled all over the world and seen places I would never imagine, except through a picture on the Internet or in a book.

My identity comes from the love I receive, the belief from others who know, encourage, and inspire me. My identity comes from my faith, from the one who created me. My identity comes from digging deep within and listening to the whisper that speaks to me. My identity comes from trusting myself. When we find our true identity, and learn to trust our gut, the oyster will open up, and another pearl will be discovered for our journey.

About the Author

Carol Shockley, founder of Shockley Event Management, skillfully creates calm from chaos throughout the planning, strategy, and management of events ranging from simple to complex and ensures that her clients are confident that their needs and vision are supported every step of the way.

Carol works hands-on with her clients to ensure clarity for the event's desired outcome. She is committed 100 percent to the success of her clients and always takes the extra steps to understand the relationship needed between the event host and attendees in order to best support the intended outcome.

This unique focus is the foundation of Shockley Event Management and has helped Carol successfully manage events across the country, including long-term, large-scale events with hundreds of volunteers and thousands of attendees and intimate venues with focused groups.

Visit her online at http://www.shockleyeventmanagement.com.

THE MAGIC OF SHOWING UP

Inara Michele

*It is never too late to be
what you might have been.*

George Eliot

It all started on a beautiful Sunday in Las Vegas. I was in my car, driving home from yoga. I had taken the long way back, through side streets, so I could have plenty of time to spend with my thoughts. Something weighed heavily on my mind, and not even a taxing yoga workout had been able to calm me.

My boss had brought someone in from the outside to do the job I'd been promised for almost a year. Furthermore, he had spoken disparagingly about my abilities to a very trusted colleague.

As I drove, my emotions ran the gamut from anger to frustration, from powerlessness to confusion.

I had more than proven myself at this job . . . I had excelled at it. Not only that, but I had already been performing all the duties of the position, adding a lot of extra work, for no extra pay.

So why was I being told to just sit there and look pretty, yet again?

This was the third time that I had excelled at a job and had been mindlessly passed over for promotion.

The funniest thing is that these weren't even things I really wanted to do. I just happened to have the drive and determination to become really good at whatever I did, whether I liked it or not.

What did it mean, that I was driven to succeed at things I did not really like and that I often got close to success but never quite arrived? And what did it say about me and who I was?

These were the thoughts that troubled my mind as I drove and absentmindedly scanned through the radio stations. For no particular reason, I stopped on a talk-radio channel . . . a bit of an odd choice, since I usually preferred to unwind and relax to music while I drove. It happened to be a local attorney's weekly radio show.

Just as I was tuning in, the host was announcing his next segment. He was going to interview a man who had toured with a couple of famous rock bands and was now a successful marketing expert.

To be quite honest, the only reason I stayed on the station was that, as a kid, I'd been a huge fan of one of the bands he'd mentioned, and I wanted to hear some behind-the-scenes stories.

The gentleman being interviewed spoke about his college days and how he had ended up as an assistant in a theater in his home town. It was a fun and exciting story, but there was something in particular that stood out.

He spoke about a time when he had gone back to the theater on his night off to take his mother backstage to meet a very famous band. He had worked the previous night and had had no intention of going in that night. But he had, at the insistence of his mother, and it had led to an offer to tour with the band that completely changed his life.

The guest had gone on to the next part of the story when the host politely interrupted him, saying he wanted to put what he'd just said into perspective for his listeners. He emphasized the point that someone could be in a seemingly mediocre job or situation, and something amazing could still happen.

That was me! I was most certainly in a mediocre situation fighting for recognition in a field I had no passion for, feeling so miserable that I had even begun to believe there was something wrong with me.

I had travelled the world, sang opera in Europe and North America, written short stories and books that remained thus far unpublished. And here I was, crying over something that had nothing to do with who I truly was or what I really wanted.

But then something even more amazing happened! The man being interviewed announced that he would be giving a free seminar in LA that weekend and that anyone who had ever wanted to write, publish, and sell a book should attend.

That stopped me in my tracks! I knew at that moment—I was certain of it—this was my chance, my opportunity to get to the life I was meant to live.

For years, I'd felt as if I was riding on the wrong train track, while the life I was really meant to live was running parallel on a different track that I just couldn't get to. I kept watching as the train of my *true* life made all the stops I was supposed to make and did all the things I was supposed to do. Meanwhile, the train I was on kept gaining speed and leading me to somewhere I did not belong. And I couldn't jump tracks. I didn't know how.

But suddenly I knew, if I could just do this, I could jump the tracks. Just like the guest's life had changed by simply showing up, I knew that if I just showed up, my life would change too!

I won't sugarcoat it. It was scary. I had just bought a house, and my savings were lower than they'd ever been in my entire adult life. I knew my boss wouldn't let me take time off, which meant I'd have to quit. And then there would be the expenses associated with travel.

But I had missed plenty of opportunities in the past and hid behind a million excuses. So I rushed home, RSVPd for the seminar and reserved my hotel room.

I spent the next week wrapping up all the loose ends at work.

As I had guessed, my boss said I most definitely could not take a weekend off. So the day before I would be driving to California, I took a deep breath and quit my job. And I am not exaggerating when I tell you that the relief was palpable; the weight off my shoulders was tangible. I can't quite explain it, but I literally felt my whole universe shift. Something snapped into place. I felt my life jump onto the right track.

And surprisingly enough, I was not scared at all. I had just left my job, with no concrete future prospects, about to go spend money I didn't have, yet I'd never felt better in my life. I walked to my car with a huge smile on my face.

Then, as if I'd needed further evidence that I was on the correct path, I heard the beep of my voice mail notification. I was still in the parking lot when I listened to the message. A representative from a company I had interviewed with a few weeks before was offering me to start the following Monday, with paid training and an incredible benefits package, working less hours for more money. Just the perfect support I would need to pursue my dreams!

To recount the events of the weekend would need many more pages than I have available here and is in itself its own story. But I can tell you what came of it: I took a half-written book and notes I'd been sitting on for over five years and got it to first draft. I wrote 75 percent of a second book and began organizing material that I had previously used to coach friends and colleagues when they came to me for advice into what will be an amazing seminar, a wonderful workshop, and an empowering system.

So why and how did this all happen?

I truly believe that my amazing career as an author and speaker got started because I had finally begun to question and rebel against the false identity I had adopted as a means to hide from my dreams and true desires. And this act of rebelling against the status quo called forth events that are nothing short of amazing: from unwittingly landing on that particular radio station to receiving a job offer before I had left for the seminar. But none of it would've meant anything if I hadn't committed to the decision to show up, no matter what.

And therein lies the magic: I chose to show up. And that in itself was a personal miracle. This wasn't the first time I'd been presented with an amazing opportunity. But somehow, all the right ingredients had come together and had inspired me to act.

By questioning my circumstances, taking a seemingly frightening chance, seizing an incredible opportunity, and just showing up, I reclaimed my true identity: The identity of a woman of power with something incredible to say and share.

And I will never again just sit there and look pretty!

About the Author

Inara Michele is an author, speaker, and female empowerment expert. She previously worked as an automotive sales and finance specialist and has extensive experience in sales. She is a professional opera singer who has performed in Europe, Latin America, and the United States—even founding her own company in Las Vegas to help professional singers find a place to workshop and display their art.

She has been speaking on the topic of female empowerment for several years, helping friends and colleagues regain their power and find fulfillment in their personal lives.

She is currently working on an amazing female empowerment system that will consist of seminars, workshops, books, and other media formats.

Inara believes that women could rule the world if they only knew how. She wants to show them how.

YOU ARE MAGNIFICENT

Maryann Ehmann

Be not another, if you can be yourself.

Paracelsus

You are magnificent, a magnificent masterpiece, here to do a magnificent work.

Sound too lofty? Too unrealistic? Doesn't fit with the image you have of yourself?

I understand. Magnificence was not a word I often used, especially when it came to describing me. But it's a word that was divinely downloaded to me one day, and as I have embraced it and made it my truth, all of heaven and earth has opened up to me.

There was a time when I was in survival mode. I was plagued with migraines, vertigo, digestive issues, and respiratory distress. We were broke, and the only thing I could see for our future was a cardboard box under a bridge that we called home. I felt powerless and out of control.

But God did a miraculous work in my mind-set, then in my body, then in our finances. I immersed myself in the study of his favor and saw how it was readily available to me and all humankind. The first major shift in my identity began: *I was highly favored and loved by God.*

As I appropriated the favor of God to myself, my perspective changed. No longer did I feel defective, inadequate, or not enough. I felt special, that I mattered, that I could handle whatever came my way.

Think about the phrase "I am . . ." Whenever we start a sentence with "I am," we are talking about identity. Unfortunately, the words that follow "I am" are not always elevating, empowering, or a fair representation of our true identity: "I'm an idiot, fat, ugly, a slug, a failure." How often do we reinforce the very things about ourselves that disempower us and move us away from our dreams and goals rather than toward them?

When we talk about the roles we play in life, while seemingly normal and neutral—that is, "I am a teacher, or a lawyer, or a coach"—they only give a picture of what it is I do. It doesn't really say much about my essence, my values, my personality, the things that make me me.

With that in mind, wouldn't we be better served if we were mindful of what we say after "I am"?

Many people worry about being themselves. Being different, "unique," was painful for me. When people laugh at you, scorn you, and even want to beat you up because you are different, there's a temptation and outright motivation to be like everyone else. The trouble was I couldn't be like everyone else. I was Asian in an all-white community. I couldn't change that. I was extra tall for a girl. I couldn't change that either. Nor could I change the fact that I had been sexually, emotionally, and physically abused. The belief that I created was "I am less than. I am worthy of mistreatment." I once believed I could not be successful being me.

I did not like being me. I often marveled at how comfortable some people were in their own skin. They had a boldness, assurance, and confidence that I lacked. Indeed, I didn't have a clue what that felt like.

But I was devoted to personal development and positivity. I read the books and did the affirmations. Like Stuart Smalley, I stared in the mirror and proclaimed over and over, "I'm smart enough. I'm good enough. And doggone it, people like me!"

But it never felt true.

It wasn't until I basked in the presence of God, studied his word about how favored I was (and we all are, by the way) for over a two-year period that I actually began to believe it.

Do you know the difference between a pickle and a cucumber? If you dipped a cucumber in a jar of pickle juice and bit into it, on the outside, it would taste like pickle juice, but on the inside, it would still taste like a cucumber.

But what if you immersed that cucumber in the pickle juice for days, weeks, even months? Eventually, no matter where you bit that pickle, it would taste like a pickle. This is what happened to me regarding the favor of God. It became a part of my essence, through and through. So much so that when I say "I am highly favored by God," I feel it in my bones. It feels like home. It feels right. This causes me to think as a highly favored person and act like one. I make choices and take risks without the fear I once had before I was pickled in favor.

Who we believe we are, consciously and subconsciously, will determine our choices, what we say, and the results we get.

If you want to know more about favor, what it is and what it isn't, you can pick up my book *Have I Ever Told You, You're My Favorite! The Importance of Feeling Special*. For me, knowing and feeling I was favored by God gave me favor with people. It opened doors and connected me with the right people, at the right time, in the right place. It catapulted my career; it brings me new clients and opportunities to speak in front of huge audiences. We all have favor with God, but knowing it will increase your courage, boldness, and joy.

I want that for you, too.

Now I thought nothing was better than favor. But seeing myself as favored was just the positioning I needed for the next upgrade in what I believed about my identity. That upgrade was *magnificence.* You see, God is all about upgrading us, from the inside out. If you pay attention, you will see his hand in directing your steps and renewing your mind, too.

As I said at the start of this chapter, you are a magnificent masterpiece, created by God to do a magnificent work on this earth. There's even a Bible verse that states as much (Ephesians 2:10). When you view yourself as magnificent, you are agreeing with God. This produces such a shift as to what you can expect in life—so much so that even miracles seem commonplace. Not that I ever want to take miracles for granted, but seeing yourself as magnificent sets you up to have a miraculous lifestyle. You see yourself as deserving it, and if you remember that you are a work of God, you do not have to fear being arrogant or boastful. You are just stating truth.

I needed to embrace favor to move forward in my dreams and fulfill the deepest desires of my heart. But magnificence goes beyond our dreams. Believing you are magnificent sets you up for a life immeasurably more so than you can even imagine.

This has happened to me. Yes, I have a dream business, making great money doing what I love, and I get to help people do the same. I travel and go to exotic places, hobnob with highly influential people, and work with powerful overcomers and high achievers. I have a stellar relationship with my children and grandchildren, who appreciate and esteem me as I do them. There was a time that I felt too small, insignificant, and lacking to have that life. Favor changed all that for me.

But magnificence has taken me to a whole new realm. You see, God has dreams for us. Dreams that are bigger than our dreams, and they are luscious dreams, ones suited perfectly for you and who you are.

I used to be afraid of the calling of God on my life. Would he ask me to go to Africa and live in a hut with a dirt floor, eating crunchy bugs and slimy worms for the sake of some poor people I did not feel connected to? I know plenty of people who have joyfully lived that kind of life. I felt guilty that I had no interest. I mistakenly thought that the more you suffered for God, the more spiritual you were, and the more pleased he was with you.

This was a result of my mistaken identity about him. With a renewed image and relationship with him, I have come to expect the wild ride of fabulous experiences, circumstances, and serendipitous moments. Not everything has to be by the book, according to plan, or following the norm. In fact, most things in my life are not! And for a former control freak, that took a bit of adjustment and a lot of trust.

There is obviously way more to the story of transformation and breakthrough than I can possibly give here in this short chapter, but seeing yourself as God sees you, favored and magnificent, is a highly empowering piece of your identity that awaits you. Getting uncomfortable to believe you are more is the kind of pain worth putting yourself through.

If I can do it, anyone can. Now go forth, oh highly favored and magnificent one! Go bask in God's favor, see yourself as magnificent, and live a life beyond your wildest dreams!

About the Author

Reinventing herself at fifty-eight, **Maryann Ehmann** believes anyone, at any age, from any circumstance, can reset their lives, have the business of their dreams, and have a lifestyle of fulfillment and freedom.

As a dream activator, breakthrough specialist, and business strategist, Maryann works with those who are committed to scaling up from mediocrity and doing whatever it takes to have a magnificent life and business. Her past experience as a prosecuting attorney, corporate manager, financial consultant, and ministry leader gives Maryann a rich background from which to draw on to help her clients and students fulfill their dreams, life purposes, and heart throbbing passions, especially in the business world.

Maryann Ehmann is the founder of Create Your Magnificent Life, a professional and personal development company. Visit her online at http://createyourmagnificentlifenow.com.

MEET THE AUTHORS

Visit http://www.DiscoverYourIBooks.com to read more about all of our wonderful authors and connect with them!

BECOME A FEATURED AUTHOR IN THE DISCOVER YOUR "I" BOOK SERIES

Real Stories from Real People to Inspire and Ignite Your Soul

This book is the first in a series of Discover Your "I" compilation anthologies. Discover Your "I" Books is a collective book project featuring real, inspirational stories from real people.

As an author, you will share your personal story of your journey from where you were to where you are now. Reveal your passion and your expertise and your struggles to your successes! If you have a story to tell that will inspire someone in some way, please consider publishing in one of our future books. You can find out more, and apply, at http://www.DiscoverYourIBooks.com.

Please watch for other books in the Discover Your "I" Book Series, or find them, at http://www.DiscoverYourIBooks.com.

A few titles include the following:

Discover Your

- *Intimacy*
- *Intuition*
- *Impact*
- *Inspiration*
- *Image*
- *Immortality*
- *Individuality*
- *Investments*
- *Intention*

Meet Sue and Susan

Sue Brooke and Susan Sheppard met at a business marketing mastermind where they discovered that their messages were not only compatible but each actually enhanced the other. They also discovered that working together, they were able to create catalytic and exponential results that neither of them could have achieved alone. The first of these endeavors is this book *Discover Your Identity.*

Sue is the founder of Discover Your "I" and co-creator of the Discover Your "I" book series. She is the owner and founder of an educational learning center in Southern California, a small-business mentor, speaker, educator, author, coach, and idea innovator! After surviving a car accident and finding herself with a depleted bank account at the age of forty-four, Sue describes "being hit by a truck" as the moment that changed her life forever. She reclaimed her identity and built successful businesses, all on her own.

Sue enjoys working with small-business owners and people who have dreams to start a business. She has the unique gift of coming up with innovative ideas and finding opportunities where no one else would think to look.

As a passionate advocate for anyone who may have lost their identity, she strives to empower and inspire them to live their passion and never to give up on their dreams, no matter how crazy they may seem!

Sue believes that everyone has a story that should be told. Giving people an avenue for sharing their own stories and encouraging others to share theirs is dream that has come to fruition in her Discover Your "I" book series.

Susan is the co-creator of the Discover Your "I" book series and founder of Getting What You Want, Inc., a life- and relationship-coaching organization created for the purpose of providing women access to the power they already have to get exactly what they want in every facet of their life. She is the author of the books

How to Get What You Want from Your Man Anytime,
Dating after 40: No More Excuses, and
Romance Re-Entry for Those Out of Practice.

Susan is a true renaissance woman who has honed her coaching skills throughout a fifty-year nursing career and twelve entrepreneurial business starts. Her business ventures stretch from construction to movie production, and include waterbed sheet sales, executive search in the oil industry, and small-business consulting for doctors and hospitals.

She has become an accomplished speaker, writer, trainer, coach, and serial entrepreneur who is passionate about true love, sacred intimacy, and getting people loved the way they want to be loved. Her primary focus these days is her Love with CLASS relationship coaching program, which when fully engaged, will guarantee anyone a significant love relationship. Susan developed her CLASS program after her divorce from the love of her life, a Vietnam vet who was a great man and a lost soul with PTSD and survivor's guilt. She took every course she could find in order to learn how to do her own love relationships better and ultimately was requested by her first client to teach what she had learned. For twenty-four years, she has entered in and out of relationship coaching with phenomenal results for singles seeking committed relationships. With an intense, straight-talking, compassionate manner, she targets your core issues and quickly moves you in the direction you want to go.

Adding publishing to her extensive experience has been a goal for years and is now coming to fulfillment

with the Discover Your "I" book series. Susan has always encouraged others around her to achieve more
than they thought they could achieve, and this series
of anthologies is another way to encourage others to
spread their wings and grow.

> *If you're living your passion, and*
> *doing what you love to do, then you've*
> *discovered who you really are!*
>
> **Sue Brooke,** ***Discover Your "I"***